# The
# Buddhic Essence

# The Buddhic Essence

## Ten Stages to Becoming a Buddha

# Elizabeth Clare Prophet

SUMMIT UNIVERSITY PRESS®

Gardiner, Montana

*The Buddhic Essence*
*Ten Stages to Becoming a Buddha*
by Elizabeth Clare Prophet
Copyright © 2009 Summit Publications, Inc.

For information, contact Summit University Press,
63 Summit Way, Gardiner, MT 59030-9314 USA
Tel: 1-800-245-5445 or 406-848-9500
www.SummitUniversityPress.com

Library of Congress Control Number: 2009925649
ISBN: 978-1-932890-16-7

SUMMIT UNIVERSITY ❧ PRESS®
Cover and book design by Lynn M. Wilbert

Printed in the United States of America
13  12  11  10  09     5  4  3  2  1

# Contents

# The Flower Sermon

Gautama Buddha taught not only through discourse and example but also, at times, through symbols and imagery. His Flower Sermon exemplifies the transmission of wisdom through direct experience.

*One day on Vulture Peak, while the disciples were seated in rapt attention, the Buddha came before the assembly and silently held up a flower. Only Mahakasyapa (Universal Light Drinker) smiled, indicating his understanding.*

*Buddha confirmed that a transmission of the Enlightened Mind had taken place without any words being spoken.*

# Introduction

*I*n this volume, Elizabeth Clare Prophet illumines our pathway to Buddhahood. Drawing upon traditional and modern Buddhist teachings, illustrations and stories, she shows how we can begin tracing the path that leads from where we are today to complete Buddhic enlightenment.

In the first half of the book, Mrs. Prophet lays the foundation for the ten stages of this path. She begins with the premise that we all contain the seed of Buddhahood, called the Buddha-nature. She describes the transcendental force of *bodhicitta,* the "cosmic will for universal salvation," and explains specific devotional practices that cultivate the conditions in which it can arise. Those who vow to attain Buddhahood for the benefit of all life are called *bodhisattvas.* Mrs. Prophet offers insight into the mind and heart of the bodhisattva and elucidates the nature of vows and their transcendent power to tether the bodhisattva to his goal. The second half of the book outlines the traditional ten stages of the bodhisattva's path to Buddhahood. Mrs. Prophet describes ten transcendental virtues the aspirant perfects along the way and offers insightful tips for developing them. She defines the "three bodies of the Buddha" the aspirant to Buddhahood merges with. And in conclusion, she explains how Buddhist mantras help us overcome obstacles to spiritual growth while increasing wisdom, compassion, forgiveness and joy.

### A PATH OF WISDOM AND COMPASSION

Gautama Buddha's discourses and dialogues are recorded in the Buddhist *sutras* (literally "threads on which jewels are strung"). Some sutras were preached directly by Gautama; others were recited by a disciple either in the Buddha's presence or under his direct inspiration. A few sutras contain the words of transcendent bodhisattvas, beings with the attainment of Buddhahood; these conclude with the Buddha's approval of the teaching they contain. Regardless of the form of delivery, the sutras are all said to emanate from the Enlightened Mind. The sutras, along with the rules of discipline and expository teachings, constitute the wisdom aspect of the Buddha's teachings.

Compassion is another hallmark of Buddhism. Those who observed Gautama Buddha's life spoke of his compassionate behavior and of the practical assistance he gave to so many. His living example of compassion constitutes an equally important aspect of his teaching.

These twin ideals of wisdom and compassion are embodied in the *bodhisattva ideal*. The bodhisattva strives to attain the wisdom of Buddhahood while compassionately dedicating himself to the salvation of all.

## IDEAL ROLE MODELS

Buddhism speaks of earthly bodhisattvas and transcendent (celestial or great) bodhisattvas. Earthly bodhisattvas strive for enlightenment while expressing altruism and compassion for others. Transcendent bodhisattvas have the attainment of a Buddha but have postponed their entry into ultimate nirvana (complete liberation) until all beings realize enlightenment. The great bodhisattvas dwell in the heaven-world, assisting and guiding us toward enlightenment, yet they can assume any physical form they desire in order to offer assistance to life. Their perfect balance of wisdom and compassion makes them ideal role models.

Manjushri is the great Bodhisattva of Wisdom, revered by Buddhists as the patron of arts and sciences and the master of eloquence. In some traditions, Manjushri is said to have become a perfectly enlightened Buddha many aeons ago in another universe. Because wisdom is essential to liberation from suffering, Manjushri is a herald of emancipation.

Kuan Yin, the Bodhisattva of Compassion, is perhaps the most well-known transcendent bodhisattva. She is at times depicted in masculine form and is known by various names, among them Avalokiteshvara and Chenrezi. According to legend, Kuan Yin was about to enter heaven but paused on the threshold as the cries of the world reached her ears. The Kuan Yin Sutra, a chapter of the Lotus Sutra, contains the Buddha's teaching on the Universal Gate of Kuan Yin. In Buddhism, a gate is an entrance to the dharma (the Buddha's teachings), a beginning toward awakening. Kuan Yin's universal gate, being immensely wide, can accommodate innumerable beings. Thus, Kuan Yin makes it possible for all to follow the path to Buddhahood.

It is our prayer that Mrs. Prophet's presentation of *The Buddhic Essence* will help you discover your own Buddhanature and will illumine the path you walk toward enlightenment and Buddhahood.

*The Editors*

# Buddhas and Immortals

A theme in ancient Buddhist literature is the creation of the world by a Mother Goddess, the Eternal Venerable Mother, who sent down to earth ninety-six myriads of her children. They were originally Buddhas and immortals, but once on earth they forgot their true home in paradise.

They grew attached to fame, profit and sensual pleasures. Trapped by these desires, they became enmeshed in samsara (the sea of suffering). And so the Great Law required them to repeatedly die and be reborn that they might recognize the transient nature of their desires.

The Venerable Mother grieved for her lost children and sent down messenger deities to remind them of their true nature and the way back home. These messengers were Buddhas who had passed all the initiations of the bodhisattvas.

It is prophesied that at the end of the time of trials the Venerable Mother's children will recover their original wholeness and be reunited. There is also the hope in this ancient literature that the world itself will be changed into a realm of perfect bliss.

*Crowned Buddha or Bodhisattva, life size, painted cloth over wood, around 350 years old.* The crown symbolizes the Buddha's sovereignty and is sometimes used to depict Buddhas in the Body of Bliss. The topknot or cranial knob (Skt. usnisa) symbolizes his wisdom, openness and spiritual dominion as an enlightened being.

# 1

## Buddha-Nature Is Universal

Within Buddhist scripture is Gautama Buddha's teaching that all beings have within them the *Buddha-nature*—the essence, or seed, of Buddhahood. We have the seed of Buddhahood right inside of us. And because we have it, we have the potential to become a Buddha.

One way I define Buddhism is "the igniting of the internal being of God." Isn't this what we are all seeking? We have the hope that somehow something inside of us can be ignited. We seek to become more than we are currently expressing. And when we become that "more," we will let go of certain things that we currently believe ourselves to be but which, in Reality, we are not.

As we study and ponder the mystical paths of the world's religions, we see that these seemingly different paths do in fact converge. It is almost as though, when we hear a teaching from one of them, we wonder whether it is from the mystical path of Buddhism or Christianity or Hinduism, Judaism or Islam or Taoism, et cetera, because we are hearing the very same things from each of them. Confirmation of the same inner spiritual path comes from many different peoples in different ages, from different languages and cultures, from different prophets and teachers. The mystical paths all come to this one and single conclusion: *that the ultimate goal of the path is union with God, with Reality, with the Absolute.*

I desire to see people liberated from having to defend their personal experiences and beliefs based on what they or others associate with a particular religion. I would like them to be able to take all of the threads of this one point that is made in the mystical path of each religion and simply know that those Hindus, Buddhists, Taoists, Jews, Christians, Muslims and others who follow a mystical path all believe this. It is wonderfully liberating to realize that not millions of people at one time but millions of people from all times and all ages have sought and realized union with God.

In this book we are going to look at the path that our beloved Gautama Buddha has developed for entering into and realizing this ultimate union.

## BECOMING THE TEACHING

An ancient Buddhist text proclaims, "The road to Buddhahood is open to all. At all times have all living beings the Germ of Buddhahood in them."[1] Tibetan lama and scholar Geshe Ngawang Wangyal writes, "There exists in each living being the potential for attaining Buddhahood, called the Buddha-essence…, the 'legacy abiding within.'… This Buddha-essence… is untainted by any defilement, existing as pure from the very beginning even though in the midst of afflictive emotions."[2]

One of Gautama's most important legacies was his message to seek nothing outside of our self, to go within and become the Buddha as he had. He took the role of guide and exemplar to show us the way. This point is illustrated with a glimpse into the life of Ananda, one of Gautama Buddha's great disciples.

Ananda, a cousin of Gautama, was his personal assistant for twenty-five years. He is said to have attended the Buddha with great devotion and to have acted with compassion toward all. Ananda's chief renown, however, is for his brilliant mind and retentive memory. It is said that he could recite from memory every sermon the Buddha had delivered. In many of the sutras that begin with the words "Thus have I heard," the speaker is Ananda.

Despite Ananda's intellectual grasp of the teaching, the Buddha scolded him for not understanding the nature of his true mind. The Surangama (Heroic Gate) Sutra records the Buddha's words:

> *You have learned the Teachings by listening to the words of Lord Buddha and then committing them to memory.*

*Why do you not learn from your own self by listening to the sound of the Intrinsic Dharma within your own Mind and then practising reflection upon it?*[3]

Through this and other instruction the Buddha gave to Ananda and others on that occasion, Ananda realized that he had not followed the injunction of the Buddha to become the teaching. The sutra records Ananda's remorse:

*After I left home to follow the Buddha, I merely relied on His transcendental power and always thought that I could dispense with practice since He would bestow samadhi upon me. I did not know that He could not be my substitute and so lost (sight of) my fundamental Mind. This is why, though I joined the Order, my mind was unable to enter the Tao. I was like a destitute son running away from his father. I only realize now that, in spite of much listening (to the Dharma), if I do not practise it, I shall come to nothing as if I had not heard it, like a man who cannot satisfy his hunger by merely speaking of food.*[4]

As the Buddha's life was drawing to a close, Ananda was grief-stricken over the impending loss and distraught with thoughts that he would have to strive for perfection without the aid of the Buddha. The Digha Nikaya records that the Buddha consoled him, saying three times, "For a long time, Ānanda, you have been very near to me by acts of love, kind and good, never varying, beyond all measure." The Buddha then urged Ananda to apply himself in earnest and said that he would soon realize emancipation.

On an occasion when another disciple teased Ananda for his lack of attainment despite his close association with the Buddha, Gautama prophesied that Ananda would attain liberation "in this very life." And he did: Buddhist records state that Ananda attained nirvana (liberation) on the eve of the First Buddhist Council, shortly after the Buddha's death.

### THE BLESSINGS OF ALL THE BUDDHAS

The fortieth chapter of the Avatamsaka (Flower Ornament) Sutra speaks of a perennial seeker named Sudhana (Good Wealth). In his search for enlightenment, Sudhana is said to have visited or studied with a total of fifty-three spiritual teachers. According to Buddhist tradition, he became the equal of the Buddhas in one lifetime.

Guidance from a spiritual director or guru (teacher) is fundamental to many religious paths, the bodhisattva path included. By the diligent practice of the teachings given by a true spiritual teacher, the disciple gains the blessings of all the Buddhas. Tibetan lama Dilgo Khyentse Rinpoche explained this principle in his book *The Wish-Fulfilling Jewel:*

> *If one sees the teacher merely as an ordinary being, then one will receive only the "blessings" of ordinary beings; if one sees him as an* arhat *[worthy one]…, then one will receive the corresponding blessings; if one sees the teacher as a bodhisattva, one will receive the blessings of the bodhisattvas. If, however, one can see the teacher as a*

*buddha, then one will receive the blessings of the buddhas.*
*[The guru] is like...a wish-fulfilling jewel granting all*
*the qualities of realization, a father and a mother giving*
*their love equally to all sentient beings, a great river of com-*
*passion, a mountain rising above worldly concerns un-*
*shaken by the winds of emotions, and a great cloud filled*
*with rain to soothe the torments of the passions. In brief,*
*he is the equal of all the buddhas. To make any connection*
*with him, whether through seeing him, hearing his voice,*
*remembering him, or being touched by his hand, will lead*
*us toward liberation. To have full confidence in him is the*
*sure way to progress toward enlightenment. The warmth*
*of his wisdom and compassion will melt the ore of our*
*being and release the gold of the buddha-nature within.*[5]

## SHAN TS'AI: THE SEARCH FOR A TEACHER

A popular legend tells of the seeker Shan Ts'ai (Virtuous
Talent), a disciple and attendant of Kuan Yin. As a youth,
Shan Ts'ai came to study under Kuan Yin when she was
embodied as Miao Shan (Wondrously Kind One), a princess
who became a bodhisattva. The legend illustrates the im-
portance of the teacher for the disciple.

*Shan Ts'ai was a crippled Indian youth who desired above*
*all to study the Buddha-dharma (the teachings of the*
*Buddha). Word reached him that a masterful Buddhist*
*teacher, Miao Shan, dwelled on the rocky island of P'u-t'o*
*and he undertook the arduous journey to that place.*

*Eventually he found Miao Shan and beseeched her to instruct him in the dharma.*

*Before accepting Shan Ts'ai as a disciple, Miao Shan determined to first test his dedication and resolve. To this end she created the illusion of three pirates brandishing swords and running uphill toward her. She fled toward the edge of a cliff with the pirates in swift pursuit.*

*Believing that his teacher was in grave danger, Shan Ts'ai hobbled up the hill to defend her. As the pirates neared Miao Shan, she jumped over the cliff's edge. The pirates quickly followed. When Shan Ts'ai reached the edge of the cliff, he crawled over, lost his balance and fell.*

*Miao Shan halted Shan Ts'ai's fall in midair. (The illusory pirates had vanished.) Miao Shan then asked Shan Ts'ai to walk, whereupon he discovered that he could walk normally and was no longer crippled. When he glanced into a pool of water, he saw that he was now handsome; his face, too, had been transformed.*

*Convinced of Shan Ts'ai's dedication, Miao Shan accepted him as a disciple and taught him the entire teaching of the Buddha.*

### PRACTICAL REASONS TO WALK THE PATH

We may not realize that we took our first steps on the path to becoming a Buddha long ago, perhaps many lifetimes ago, and that we are simply picking up the path from where we left off. But whether or not we desire to become a Buddha, there are practical reasons to apply ourselves to the disciplines of this path.

On a personal level, those who strive to master the steps that lead to Buddhahood may win their freedom from the rounds of rebirth at the end of their present life or at least be reborn in better circumstances for spiritual evolution in their next life.

From a global perspective, we understand that the circumstances of life that we and future generations will see tomorrow depend on our decisions and actions today. All of the enlightened ones that have ever lived on this earth have come to bring about changes for the better. They have come to relieve the sorrowful situations that we find in this world, to bind up the wounds of mankind, to heal the brokenhearted, to ameliorate the problems of race and other misunderstandings, to give the children of this world a better future. They have come and they are still here working with mankind.

We have an opportunity to mark this moment as the point in time when we looked to the future and realized that what we plant now will be here for all who come after us. They will inherit the earth, they will inherit the consequences of what we do, and they will see the result of the vision we had when we embarked upon this path. The actions we take today will have repercussions far into the future. So today is our opportunity to dedicate ourselves to bringing this earth into a golden age.

*Reflection on the Essence*

- *What is your vision of the future for yourself, your loved ones, and for the earth?*

- *What contribution would you desire to make toward the achievement of your vision?*

- *What one small step (whether an action or a preliminary step) could you commit to today that would plant a seed toward the unfolding of your vision?*

*The bodhisattva Prince Siddhartha Gautama under the Bo tree on the night of his enlightenment.* His right hand forms the bhumisparsa mudra (earth-touching gesture), with which he defeated the Tempter Mara and his armies. As Gautama touched the earth, the earth thundered: "I bear you witness!" whereupon Mara fled.

## 2

# The Birth of the Bodhisattva Path in You

After Gautama Buddha attained enlightenment under the Bo tree, he traveled throughout India for forty-five years preaching his doctrine of the way to liberation. The path he outlined is the Middle Way, a balanced path that avoids extremes of self-indulgence and self-mortification.

Through his discourses and living example, Gautama taught a path of wisdom and compassion. He taught his disciples to devote themselves to applying the teaching and spreading it so that others might also realize the Buddha-nature within. In Mahayana Buddhism, this dual focus on self and others is called the *bodhisattva ideal*. In fact, the term Mahayana (Great Vehicle) has become synonymous with the path of the bodhisattva.

A *bodhisattva* (literally "a being of enlightenment") is one destined for Buddhahood whose energy and power is directed toward enlightenment. Yet out of deep compassion for the plight of the world and an intense yearning to save it, the bodhisattva vows to forgo ultimate nirvana until all beings are liberated.

## TO STIR THE NOBLE OF HEART

The Mahayana school believes that enlightenment is only possible by following Gautama on the bodhisattva path. As Buddhist scholar D. T. Suzuki writes, "Mahâyânism is not contented to make us mere transmitters or 'hearers' of the teachings of the Buddha, it wants to inspire with all the religious and ethical motives that stirred the noblest heart of Çâkyamuni [Gautama] to its inmost depths."[1]

Those who truly recognize that the Buddha-nature is present in all beings are filled with the desire to spread the teachings in order to awaken it in them. Buddhist teacher Nikkyo Niwano writes that "Shakyamuni himself became the Buddha by virtue of awareness of the buddha-nature of all human beings and by persevering cultivation of this awareness."[2]

## WHAT DOES A BODHISATTVA LOOK LIKE?

During a visit to America, the Sixteenth Karmapa, the spiritual head of the Karma Kagyu tradition of Tibetan

Buddhism, is reported to have shared this hint regarding modern-day bodhisattvas living in the West: "There are a lot of them. They are all over the place. But they are difficult to recognize. They are not necessarily going to look like me. They are not necessarily going to have a shaven head, wear the robes of a Buddhist monk, and so on."[3]

## A DEEPER UNDERSTANDING OF LOVE

This story about a woman from a past century provides a glimpse into what a bodhisattva might look like today:

*She was the youngest of a large, talented family. Though she herself had considerable talent, she chose to forgo her own career in order to devote herself to meditation and prayer for her brothers and sisters and to also help them in other practical ways.*

*As a child she had learned that through expanding the flame of love in her heart she could promote within others a heightened awareness that supported the blossoming of their talent. She continued this practice for many years and each of her siblings did make a contribution in their field.*

*She said that while it might seem to others that she had accomplished little, her understanding of love had deepened through her service to life. In seeing the accomplishments of her brothers and sisters, her joy was full.*

## LIVING THE TEACHING BY NURTURING OTHERS

The most humble people do not realize how much grace and light they have. I had an aunt in Switzerland who, after her husband died, ran a boarding house. Though she had little, she would take in any beggar that would come to her door, feed him and give him a night's rest. She never turned away anyone.

This humble woman was barely literate, and in the eyes of my Swiss relatives she was the lowliest of them all. Yet she truly lived the teachings. Her example taught me a great lesson: to welcome everyone, to give away all, and to nurture people. That is how to get into the unity of Being in God.

## INSPIRATION FOR THE PATH

What inspires someone to devote himself to attaining Buddhahood for the salvation of all beings? I can tell you what inspires me—and what inspires me is to know that the living God is imprisoned inside of you and that your soul is also bound because that God is imprisoned in you. And I rejoice to see the soul go free and the God flame be unlocked so that you can literally explode into the God-free being that you really are.

This, for me, is the great joy of living. If I can't help someone unlock the God inside of himself, then what good is everything else that I might do for that person?

## WHO CAN BE CALLED A BODHISATTVA?

In the simplest sense of the word, you can be called a bodhisattva from the very first moment your heart turns to the desire to be a disciple of Lord Gautama Buddha.

The moment you set yourself on the path of union with God, you can be called a bodhisattva. So don't let the thought that a bodhisattva has a certain level of attainment exclude you from this circle. You are a bodhisattva from this moment on if you desire to be.

*Reflection on the Essence*

- *What inspires you about the bodhisattva path?*

- *If you were to spend one day as a bodhisattva, how would you use that day?*

***Serene in Meditation.*** *This face detail clearly shows the urna, the dot in the middle of the forehead, above and between the eyes. It symbolizes insight and wisdom and indicates an individual with levels of enhanced perception. It is also one of the physical characteristics of a Buddha.*

# 3

Bodhicitta: Awakening the
Heart of Enlightenment

The inspiration to walk the bodhisattva path and to
attain Buddhahood for the benefit of all begins with a
spiritual awakening—an awakening of the heart and mind.
The Sanskrit term for this spiritual rebirth is *bodhicitta,* which
is usually rendered as "awakened mind" or "the thought of
enlightenment."

Bodhicitta combines the attributes of the crown chakra
and the heart chakra—Intelligence-Heart. It has also been
referred to as the "heart-of-wisdom" and "the divine spark of
the Buddha-nature in the heart."[1] Ananda Coomaraswamy,
a historian of Indian culture and religion, wrote:

> There is...[a] side to conscience which impels the indi-
> vidual...to expend himself [for others'] advantage, in
> accordance with the principle that Love can never be idle:

*this is... the Bodhi-citta, or Heart of Enlightenment.... It does not arise from reflection, but from the harmony of the individual will with the wisdom and activity of the Buddhas. This condition is sometimes spoken of... as a state of grace, or more popularly as the state of 'being in tune with the Infinite.'... The awakening of the bodhi-citta is poetically represented in Buddhist literature as the opening of the lotus of the heart.*[2]

Nagarjuna, an ancient Buddhist philosopher, explained that "one who understands the nature of the Bodhicitta sees everything with a loving heart, for love is the essence of the Bodhicitta. The Bodhicitta is the highest essence. Therefore, all Bodhisattvas find their raison d'être of existence in this great loving heart."[3]

A DYNAMIC COSMIC FORCE

In essence, bodhicitta can be seen as a dynamic cosmic force. Nagarjuna taught that there is only one bodhicitta, an active universal force that arises and expresses itself to varying degrees and in various ways in individuals. He said, "The Bodhicitta, abiding in the heart of sameness... creates individual means of salvation.... One who understands this heart becomes emancipated from the dualistic view of birth and death and performs such acts as are beneficial both to oneself and to others."[4]

Buddhists sometimes explain the nature of bodhicitta by comparing it to the moon: Just as the moon is reflected variously in different bodies of water but remains a single orb, so bodhicitta has many and varied manifestations yet remains a single force.

## THE POTENTIAL SPARK OF ILLUMINATION WITHIN

Tibetan Buddhist scholar Lama Anagarika Govinda speaks of bodhicitta as the "potential spark of Illumination within us." He writes:

> *The discovery of this spark is the beginning of the* Bodhisattva-*Path, which achieves the liberation from suffering and from the fetters of egohood not by a negation of life, but by service to our fellow-beings, while striving towards Perfect Enlightenment....*
>
> Bodhi-citta *is...the spark of that deeper consciousness, which in the process of enlightenment is converted from a latent into an active all-penetrating and radiating force. Before this awakening has taken place, our existence is a senseless running about in circles; and since we cannot find any meaning within ourselves, the world around us appears equally meaningless....*
>
> *If...we take the view that consciousness is not a product of the world, but that the world is a product of consciousness..., it becomes obvious that we live in exactly the type of world which we have created and therefore deserved, and that the remedy cannot be an 'escape' from the 'world' but only a change of 'mind'. Such a change, however, can only take place, if we know the innermost nature of this mind*

*and its power. A mind which is capable of interpreting the rays of heavenly bodies, millions of light-years distant, is not less wonderful than the nature of light itself. How much greater is the miracle of that inner light, which dwells in the depths of our consciousness!*

*... Thus there can be only one problem for us: to awaken within ourselves this deeper consciousness and to penetrate to that state, which the Buddha called the 'Awakening' or 'Enlightenment'. This is the* Bodhisattva-Mārga *[bodhisattva path], the way to the realization of Buddhahood within ourselves.*[5]

A CONVERSION EXPERIENCE

The arousing of bodhicitta is a conversion experience, an awakening—the aspiration for enlightenment for the sake of all life. It is a spiritual catalyst for total personal transformation and is thus said to turn one's life upside down. Like the philosopher's stone, that substance believed by alchemists to have the capacity to transform base metals into gold, bodhicitta transforms the base metal of our human karma of defiled thought into the pure gold of perfect wisdom.

Govinda explains that bodhicitta "converts all the elements of consciousness into means or tools of Enlightenment" and says this transformation occurs when we first become conscious of our capacity for enlightenment. He writes, "He who has found the Philosopher's Stone, the radiant jewel *(mani)* of the enlightened mind *(bodhi-citta)* within his own heart, transforms his mortal consciousness into that of immortality, perceives the infinite in the finite and turns *Saṁsāra* into *Nirvāṇa*."[6]

## A WORLD-ENGULFING CONFLAGRATION

Bhikshu Sangharakshita, a Buddhist priest and scholar, speaks of bodhicitta as a profound spiritual experience that reorients a devotee's complete existence, being and nature. He writes:

> [The] attainment of Supreme Buddhahood apart, the Rising of the Thought of Enlightenment...is the most important event that can occur in the life of a human being. As by the discovery of a priceless jewel a poor man becomes immensely rich, so with the Rising of the Thought of Enlightenment the devotee is transformed into a Bodhisattva....[7]
>
> Bodhicitta is not a phenomenon which arises once at the beginning of a Bodhisattva's career and then subsides: like a tiny spark that develops from a flame into a world-engulfing conflagration, it grows as [the Bodhisattva] progresses.[8]

## MIAO SHAN: UNSHAKABLE DIRECTNESS TOWARD THE GREAT GOAL

The popular legend of Miao Shan, an embodiment of Kuan Yin, illustrates the arising of bodhicitta "from a flame into a world-engulfing conflagration." Miao Shan demonstrates the bodhisattva's unshakable resolve toward the great goal of universal enlightenment.

*The princess Miao Shan desired above all to lead a life of pious contemplation. Her father, a king who had no sons, was determined that she and her two sisters should marry highly accomplished men, each of whom would have the potential to rule his kingdom. The king initially agreed to let Miao Shan enter the White Sparrow Convent, thinking that a child accustomed to royal comforts would soon weary of austerities. To accelerate his plan, he instructed the convent authorities to treat her severely, yet even the harshest treatment failed to dissuade Miao Shan from her goal. Enraged, the king ordered that the princess be executed.*

*According to one version of the story, as Miao Shan knelt before the executioner, she mercifully volunteered to take upon herself the massive karma he would generate by killing her. Just then, however, an enormous tiger appeared and bore the girl away. The trembling onlookers considered that the local guardian deity had intervened to save the innocent princess.*

Author John Blofeld tells what happened next:

*From a cavern in the hills, whither the deity had borne her, the Princess Miao Shan now descended into hell and there, by the power of her unsullied purity, compelled its ruler to release every one of the shivering wretches delivered to him for punishment in requital of their evil deeds.... [For] who could forbear the sweet pleading of a princess who valued purity more than life itself?*

*Returning to the dwelling of the tutelary [guardian] deity, Miao Shan received the signal honour of a visit from Amitabha Buddha in person!...He abjured her to seek safety on...the Island of P'u-t'o. 'Around that isle, dear child, lies a dragon-haunted ocean into which none but the pure in heart, least of all your father, dare set sail. There you will be able to devote both day and night to blissful meditation and thus at last attain your pious wish to become a Bodhisattva empowered to succor errant beings....' So saying, the Buddha withdrew.*

*An island deity, summoned from Potala, carried the princess to her new abode, travelling more swiftly than the wind. For nine full years Miao Shan, when not engaged in meditation, performed deeds of compassion which, crowning the merits acquired in previous lives, completed all that remained to enable her to attain the status of Bodhisattvahood.*[9]

### SEEDS OF VIRTUE, ROOTS OF MERIT

An individual may have seeds of virtue planted in his mind by hearing the teaching of a Buddha or a bodhisattva. As these seeds are tended through many lifetimes of study and spiritual practice, they grow into roots of merit. By the

grace of hearing the teaching and the merit of responding
to the teacher, the devotee is eventually able to generate
bodhicitta.

### LUNG NÜ: RESPONDING TO THE TEACHER

The legend of Lung Nü (Dragon Maiden) illustrates this
point. The story tells how the maiden, the granddaughter of
a dragon king (a water deity who governs a body of water),
came to devote her life to the bodhisattva path.

*One day the bodhisattva Miao Shan heard a cry of distress
and saw that the son of a dragon king, while exploring the
sea in the form of a fish, had been caught by a fisherman
and was now being carried to market. She knew that as
long as the unfortunate being remained on land, he would
be trapped in the fish form and powerless to escape.*

*Acting immediately, Miao Shan gave her disciple
Shan Ts'ai a purse filled with money and instructed him
to purchase the fish and return it to the sea. He arrived at
the market to find that a large crowd had already gathered, excited by the news that a fish caught many hours
earlier was still so lively. Convinced that by eating such a
fish one might gain immortality, the crowd bid higher and
higher for it and Shan Ts'ai was outbid.*

*He then begged the fishmonger to spare the life of
the fish. At that moment, from far away, Miao Shan's
voice rang clear above the noisy crowd, saying that one
who attempts to save a life has a greater claim than one*

who attempts to take it. All arguing ceased. The fish was given to Shan Ts'ai and he returned it safely to the sea, where it resumed its true form.

The dragon king, to express his gratitude, sent his granddaughter Lung Nü to present to Miao Shan his treasured Night Brilliance Pearl. The precious jewel shone so brightly that, no matter how dark the night, one could read the sacred scriptures by its light.

Lung Nü was deeply moved by the presence and virtue of Miao Shan and asked to remain with her in order to study the Buddha dharma. She also vowed at that time to dedicate herself to becoming a bodhisattva. Miao Shan accepted the dragon maiden as a disciple, and from that time forward Lung Nü has remained in the bodhisattva's service.

Kuan Yin with Shan Ts'ai
and Lung Nü

## Reflection on the Essence

- *What experiences or moments in your past have given deeper meaning to your life?*

- *In your life at present, what motivates you—what inspires you or gives your life meaning? (This could be something you are presently doing, a cherished aspiration, or something you catch a glimpse of when you are in communion with your inner being.)*

- *What could you do today toward making that cherished dream or activity a bigger or more fulfilling part of your life?*

# 4

*Six Practices of Supreme Worship*

The arising of bodhicitta within an aspirant is not an event of one day; the devotee's preparation can span lifetimes. Neither is bodhicitta's arising a matter of chance. Bodhicitta is believed to be inherent within all, but it lies dormant until nurtured by spiritual practice. Sangharakshita says:

> It is one of the most fundamental principles of Buddhist thought...that whatever arises in the world,...at any level, arises in dependence on causes and conditions.... The emergence of the Bodhicitta within us...depends upon the creation of certain mental and spiritual conditions.... And when we create them, the Bodhicitta will then arise.[1]

## SHANTIDEVA'S DEVOTIONAL PRACTICES

Shantideva (Divine Peace), an eighth-century Buddhist monk and sage who is revered as a bodhisattva, outlined six devotional practices he considered essential to supreme worship. These practices are recorded in his landmark work, *Bodhicharyavatara* (The Way of the Bodhisattva):

1. *Offerings and Adoration: Giving oneself in adoration of the Buddhas, great bodhisattvas and the dharma.*

2. *Taking Refuge in the Three Jewels—the Buddha (the Teacher), the Dharma (the Teaching), and the Sangha (the Spiritual Community of the Buddha).*

3. *Confession: Discovering the power of regret.*

4. *Rejoicing in the Merits of Others: Celebrating the merits, virtues and attainments of others.*

5. *Prayer and Supplication: Requesting the enlightened ones to preach the dharma and not pass into nirvana.*

6. *Dedication of Merit: Application of merit to the welfare of others.*

Following are reflections on how we can incorporate the essence of these six devotional practices into our daily life in preparation for the arising of bodhicitta in us.

1. **Offerings and Adoration.** In his discourse, Shantideva dedicates several verses to offering to the Buddhas and great bodhisattvas the beauties of nature—flowers and fruits, gem-encrusted mountains, heavenly trees, the beautiful cry of wild geese—"all these unowned gifts from the limitless spheres of space." Then he offers that which means the most: himself. "In all of my lifetimes I shall offer all my bodies to the buddhas and their sons. Please accept me, O noble warriors, as I reverently become your subject and follow your advice. Protected by your power I shall remain unafraid…and shall benefit others."[2]

   **Opening a stream of light.** Adoration is always of the flame of the heart of the Lord within, who is consecrated and dedicated in (i.e., one with) the Buddhas and bodhisattvas. When we are in a state of profound worship and gratitude, concentrating fully on God, nothing can vie in that moment for our attention. Our devotion opens a tremendous stream of light whereby we direct light to God and God returns it to us multiplied.

   It doesn't matter what church or temple or mosque we attend or whether we commune in nature or in another setting. It doesn't matter whether we sing hymns, chant mantras or worship in some other way. What matters is that we are communing in our heart with God. And each time we do this, we and God meet in that sacred space that we have created by our devotion. We are pursuing God, and God is pursuing us.

2. **Taking Refuge in the Three Jewels.** The Three Jewels of Buddhism are the Buddha (the Teacher), the Dharma (the Teaching), and the Sangha (the Spiritual Community of the Buddha). Buddhist rituals and functions include the taking of refuge in these three absolutes, which is done through the offering of a spoken prayer. This popular version of the refuge prayer helps illumine its meaning and scope:

> *We take refuge in the Buddha*
> *And pray that together with all living beings*
> *We understand the substance of the Great Way*
> *And the supreme awakened mind.*
>
> *We take refuge in the Dharma*
> *And pray that together with all living beings*
> *We enter deeply the treasury of sutras*
> *With wisdom like the ocean.*
>
> *We take refuge in the Sangha*
> *And pray that together with all living beings*
> *Together in truth*
> *The people will be without obstruction.*

**The guru represents the lineage of teachers.** In Tibetan Buddhism, the refuge prayer begins with the words "I take refuge in the guru (or gurus)." A true guru, as the Buddha's representative and the transmitter of his teaching, embodies the Three Jewels. The term *guru* encompasses not only the embodied teacher but the entire lineage of teachers that have preceded and come after Gautama Buddha as well as the office and mantle of Guru.

**Gaining fearlessness.** The Maha-parinirvana (Perfect Quietude) Sutra states that by taking refuge in the Three Jewels, fearlessness is gained. I have found that this fearlessness comes from comprehending the all-power, the all-protection of these absolutes. Gautama Buddha bears the flame of fearless compassion. We gain fearlessness through taking refuge because by so doing we become one with the Buddha, the guru (as the Buddha's representative), the dharma and the sangha. When we become one with them, we unite with that supremacy of being and can have confidence that we are therefore sealed by and within them.

**Developing trust.** Trust is such a basic element of the path. If we cannot trust the Buddha (and the Buddha in the guru), if we cannot trust the teaching, if we cannot trust the community, then can we trust ourselves? Who or what can we trust if we cannot trust these three that are provided for our strengthening and for our safety? If we do not have trust, then let's go to the root of our mistrust and the karmic conditions that caused it, however far back; heal the cause, effect, record and memory of it; and begin anew to trust God and to trust the God in ourselves.

Buddhist teacher Geshe Gyatso offers this analogy:

*What is the necessity of going for refuge to these three objects? If a sick person is to get well again, he or she must rely upon a skillful physician, effective medicine and sympathetic and attentive nurses. In the same way, sentient beings caught up in the vicious circle of cyclic existence (Skt. samsara) are all afflicted by the sickness of their delusions, having found nothing in which they can take refuge. Only by entrusting themselves to the perfect physician: the buddha, the medicine of dharma and the sangha nurses will they ever be cured of their ailments. Therefore if there is to be an end to our dissatisfaction and suffering we must all discover and entrust ourselves to these three precious and sublime jewels.*[3]

3.   **Confession.** The practice of confession dates back to early Buddhism. Sangharakshita writes that in some Buddhist lands

*monks who have been spending their 'rainy season retreat' at the same monastery or who for any other reason have been living together still honor the ancient custom of begging each other's pardon for any fault of which they might have been guilty during this period. Disciples taking leave of their masters recite a Pali stanza asking forgiveness for whatever sins they might have committed by means of body, speech or mind.*[4]

The mystics of the religions of East and West all come to an awareness of the inner, all-engulfing light. By that light they see the inadequacy of the human condition and they desire to confess it, thereby to cast it into the sacred fire. Repentance, confession of sin and then asking for and accepting forgiveness allows the soul to be renewed in the flame of innocence.

**A ritual for casting sin into the sacred fire.** We can symbolically cast our sins into the sacred fire by writing them in a letter that we burn. We offer our confession to the Holy of holies upon the altar of our being, including sins from past lives going back to the moment we left the state of oneness with God.

This can be a ritual we engage in each night as we prepare for bed: kneeling in prayer, reviewing our day, calling on the law of forgiveness, and putting into the sacred fire all that never should have been. If we know that we require a penance or we wish to perform one, we can offer a specific service or prayers daily for a time as that penance.

**A key to joy, happiness and freedom.** By confessing our sins and balancing the karma for them, we keep ourselves right with God. When we do this, there is not even the thickness of a thin piece of paper separating us from God. We are one with God.

This is a key to joy, happiness and freedom. It's the key whereby we can love everyone we see and speak

with because we know that God is in us. We can love
the God in ourselves because we're settling our accounts
daily with God. And because we can love the God in
ourselves, we can love the God in all people.

I invite you to try putting it all into the flame each
day. Then see what happens in your life.

4. **Rejoicing in the Merits of Others.** Rejoicing in others'
merits, virtues and attainments means affirming and
confirming their accomplishments. If we perceive another's merit to be greater than ours, we can say to ourselves, "What man has done, man can do." And if we or
others have done things that are not right, then we can
say, "What man has done, he can undo by the violet
flame." By equalizing the flow of energy between ourselves and others, the violet flame helps us to rejoice in
their merits.

**Increasing joy and fulfillment with the violet flame.**
The violet flame is a spiritual fire of mercy and forgiveness that acts like a miracle solvent. The violet flame
vibrates at the highest frequency, dissolving negative
energies and helping us to clear the records of past
karma, thus balancing our debts to life. It helps us overcome habit patterns that make us vulnerable to suffering and interfere with our realization of our full
potential. By freeing us from limiting thoughts, feelings
and behaviors, the violet flame brings a sense of freedom, joy and fulfillment. Here's how it works:

**Changing negative energy into positive energy.** All of us, at one time or another, have misused God's energy by tying it up in negative thoughts and feelings. For example, we may have compared our accomplishments to those of others and then felt bad about ourselves or resentful or covetous of another's achievement. Negative energy of any kind, whether conscious or below the surface, can subtly influence our relationships and the way we approach situations, challenges and goals. It weighs us down and keeps us from oneness with God.

When we invoke the violet flame through the repetition of mantras, such as Kuan Yin's mantra *Om Mani Padme Hum,* we change negative energy into positive energy. This is called transmutation. As we continue giving violet flame mantras and transmuting negative energy, we are liberated to experience feelings of joy, hope, renewal and freedom.

5. **Prayer and Supplication.** When we pray, we go into another compartment of consciousness. We enter into the inner sanctuary of the heart, our private meditation room, where we commune with God and the enlightened ones. We begin by telling God how much we love him and we send intense gratitude for the blessings we have received.

**Opening the windows of consciousness.** By affirming the grace that we have received from God, we open the windows of our consciousness to receive more of his magnificent light. Then we can offer our prayers and supplications to God and to all the great beings of light to stay with us, show us the way, and preach the dharma.

6. **Dedication of Merit.** The bodhisattva offers his merit for the welfare of others. Because we have the Presence of God within us there is no limit to the effect our prayers can have. We multiply the good our prayers accomplish by the Law of the One, which is based on the unity of Being. Though there are numberless souls evolving in the duality of time and space, in Reality there is but one soul, one Buddha, one God. The duality of being, though real within the relativity of time and space, does not contradict the essential unity of God in the Absolute.

**Multiplication by the Law of the One.** On a practical level, this means that as we pray for ourselves or for one person who is sick or dealing with a particular situation, we can pray for everyone on earth who has that same sickness or is in a similar situation. We can do this with anything. For example, we can take notes on news headlines and then, in our prayer and meditation, visualize sending the spiritual fire of mercy and forgiveness, the violet flame, to those situations and others like them around the world. The violet flame can be used for every problem we are dealing with and every problem that comes to our attention.

**Directing God's light through prayer.** The Presence of God within us is what allows us to direct God's light through our prayers and call to God for divine justice, mercy and forgiveness. We do this with absolute peace and God-harmony and then we submit our prayers to the will of God and let go of the matter. We don't have to know the outcome of our prayers. God knows the secrets of all hearts and he is unerring in his judgments.

~ ~ ~

These six devotional practices cultivate within us the conditions in which bodhicitta can arise. Devotion is love, and love opens highways to God. And on the return current of the highways we build to God through prayer and mantra, light returns to us multiplied for the blessing of life.

## Reflection on the Essence

- Which one of Shantideva's devotional practices are you most drawn to trying? In what way could regular practice of it improve your well-being and help those you love?

- What action could you take today to fit one of these practices into your daily life? If you are already doing this, in what way might you improve your practice?

# 5

## The Bodhisattva Vow

The devotee's ongoing practice of supreme worship cultivates the conditions in which bodhicitta can arise within him. With the arising of bodhicitta, he is inspired to take the bodhisattva vow.

Taking the vow is not a requirement and Buddhist teachers caution individuals to recognize the difference between compassionate caring and the bodhisattva's unending aspiration toward universal salvation. Yet they also comment that those who do take the bodhisattva vow say their decision was a turning point on their path.

### FOR THE SAKE OF ONE LIVING SOUL

There are numerous versions of the bodhisattva vow, but in essence they all contain this universal formula: *So long as there remains a single being who has not been liberated,*

*I vow that I will not enter into final nirvana.*

Why is a single being of such great concern that the bodhisattva will vow, for the sake of even one living soul, to stay here to the end? It is because that living soul has the potential to be God. It was the desire to release the Buddha-nature imprisoned in flesh that long ago spurred Lord Maitreya to take his vow:

> *I saw my God imprisoned in flesh. I saw the Word imprisoned in hearts of stone. I saw my God interred in souls bound to the ways of the wicked. And I said…:*
> *I will not leave thee, O my God!*
> *I will tend that fire.*
> *I will adore that flame.*
> *And by and by some will aspire to be with me.*[1]

### THE FOUR GREAT VOWS

Whether or not bodhicitta has arisen—something which in the early stages is said to be impossible to ascertain—many Buddhists recite the bodhisattva vow as an expression of their deep commitment to the liberation of all life. The vows most commonly offered by Buddhists are the Four Great Vows, which may be stated quite simply: *May I deliver all beings from difficulties. May I eradicate all passions. May I master all dharmas. May I lead all beings to Buddhahood.*

Here is another version of the Four Great Vows that many Buddhists offer daily:

*However innumerable beings are, I vow to save them;*
*However inexhaustible the passions are,*
     *I vow to extinguish them;*
*However immeasurable the dharmas are,*
     *I vow to master them;*
*However incomparable the Buddha-truth is,*
     *I vow to attain it.*

## VOWS EXPRESS PERSONAL INTERESTS

The vows of a bodhisattva represent his personal interests. They are his individual expression of the universal force of bodhicitta. Although we may refer to the bodhisattva vow in the singular, in practice the vows are often plural. Sangharakshita elaborates:

*The vows reflect the Bodhisattva's special interests and aptitudes within the context...of the Bodhicitta and the wider framework of the Bodhisattva ideal itself....*

*... The Bodhisattva himself is like a glass prism, and the Bodhicitta is like pure white light shining through the prism. And the vows of the Bodhisattva are like the different coloured lights which emerge from the prism on the other side.... This pure, white light of this one Bodhicitta, shines through hundreds, and through thousands of individual prisms. And as it shines through them all each one produces its own particular set, its own particular combination, of colours....*

*...Any individual Bodhisattva, the scriptures make
this quite clear, is free to formulate his own set of vows,
if he or she so wishes, in accordance with his or her own
particular aspirations, within of course the general framework of the Bodhisattva Ideal itself. The main consider-
ation is that the vow should be universal in scope.*[2]

### THE VOW PROPELS US TO ITS FULFILLMENT

The bodhisattva vow affects not only this life but also
successive incarnations. This is a wondrous thing. The vow
itself becomes the force that propels the bodhisattva, lifetime
after lifetime, to its ultimate fulfillment in supreme enlightenment and Buddhahood.

We can visualize our vow as an anchor that we cast into
the deep of our Higher Mind. Then when the storms of life
rage and old thoughts and feelings surface to pull us this way
and that, our vow holds us to our inner resolve and keeps us
right with God. This is why we take vows to begin with.

The vow is like a star in our heart with a string attached
to it. God holds the other end of that string and keeps pull-
ing us forward by our vow. When we have a vow in our heart,
we have God in our heart and we have the strength of the
dharma in our heart.

A vow is the greatest protection we can ever have because that vow is truly God's energy in manifestation. Our
vow is an entering in to God, and it is God entering in to us.
Our vow is a promise that we do not break, for we under-

stand that we have made this vow directly to God's heart and in so doing have evoked from his heart a commensurate measure of support.

## STARTING WITH A SMALL COMMITMENT

Before making a vow, we can write a letter to God saying, "God, this is what I want to do for you. Please strengthen me so that I can fulfill what I want to fulfill for you." We can test ourselves first by making a promise to God for a month or a year and then seeing if for that period of time we keep that promise.

It helps not to make the hurdle too high to start with, so we take on something that's a bit difficult but that we are fairly certain we can do. From there we move on to more and more difficult commitments. Once we've kept our vow for a sustained period, we will be like steel. We will not be moved to break our vow.

## STAYING WITHIN THE CIRCLE OF GOD

What can you do if you should lapse in observing your vow? If you make a vow to God and then unwittingly or unthinkingly break it, that does not make you a miserable sinner. Never be ashamed to go back to the altar and say, "God, I have broken my vow. I want to make this right." Spend fifteen minutes or a half hour in prayer and communion with God. Ask God to send his bodhisattvas to help strengthen your determination, energy, power and will to never go back on your vow again. And then be done with it. God forgives you even before you ask him for forgiveness.

As long as you condemn yourself, you are outside of the circle of God. If you have things that you condemn yourself for, go to your altar and confess them. If you condemn yourself again, go back to the altar and confess again. Get counseling. Look at your psychology, your childhood, your parents, and so forth. Call on the law of forgiveness every time you condemn yourself. Then you'll be able to jump right back into the circle of God.

## *Reflection on the Essence*

- *In what ways does understanding of promises and vows and staying within the circle of God help you on your spiritual path?*

- *The best way to see how taking a vow works is to try it. What can you think of in this moment, no matter how small, to begin with?*

- *If you choose to do this, check back with yourself at regular intervals to assess your progress, self-correct if necessary, and recommit to your vow or promise.*

# 6

*Bodhisattvas Who Would Become a Buddha*

o illustrate the nature of the bodhisattva's aspiration to become a Buddha for the benefit of all life,
I would share with you two ancient expressions of the vow
that have illumined the way for countless bodhisattvas over
many centuries.

## TEN GREAT VOWS FROM THE DASHABHUMIKA SUTRA

The first vows we'll look at are from the Dashabhumika
(Ten Stages) Sutra. They are one of several sets of vows that
are called great vows. The Dashabhumika, a treatise on the
ten stages of the bodhisattva path, is the twenty-sixth chapter of the Avatamsaka Sutra.

These ten vows are not associated with the ten stages
themselves. Rather, they demonstrate the depth and breadth
of the vows a bodhisattva might make as he prepares to walk
the first of the ten stages of this path to Buddhahood.

1.  *To provide for the worship of all the Buddhas without exception.*

2.  *To maintain the religious Discipline that has been taught by all the Buddhas and to preserve the teaching of the Buddhas.*

3.  *To see all the incidents in the earthly career of a Buddha.*

4.  *To realise the Thought of Enlightenment [bodhicitta], to practise all the duties of a bodhisattva, to acquire all the paramitas [perfections, transcendental virtues] and purify all the stages of his career.*

5.  *To mature all beings and establish them in the knowledge of the Buddha, viz. all the four classes of beings who are in the six states of existence.*

6.  *To perceive the whole Universe.*

7.  *To purify and cleanse all the buddha-fields.*

8.  *To enter on the Great Way and to produce a common thought and purpose in all bodhisattvas.*

9.  *To make all actions of the body, speech and mind fruitful and successful.*

10. *To attain the supreme and perfect Enlightenment and to preach the Doctrine.*[1]

PRACTICAL APPLICATION OF THE VOWS

Following are my reflections on the ten vows from the Dashabhumika. Don't be surprised if you discover that you are already observing some of these vows. Or perhaps you'll feel drawn to begin observing one or more, or be inspired to formulate promises or vows of your own. As you progress along your path, you will naturally refine your spiritual practice and expression.

1. **"To provide for the worship of all the Buddhas without exception."** When we make worship a part of our daily life, we meet and commune with the Buddhas and enlightened ones. It often works best if we pick a regular time that we can commit to being at our altar each day without distraction or interruption. Then we spend whatever time we can give—five or ten minutes, a half hour or longer. What's important is that we do it regularly and daily.

2. **"To maintain the religious Discipline that has been taught by all the Buddhas and to preserve the teaching of the Buddhas."** We are preserving the teachings of the Buddhas and the great masters day by day as we live their teaching to the best of our ability. The guidelines for right living taught by the Buddha are in essence the same principles that are taught by all the enlightened ones of East and West.

3. **"To see all the incidents in the earthly career of a Buddha."** Studying the lives of the great masters and bodhisattvas who have gone before us gives us a sense of the right way to conduct ourselves and to live. The jataka tales tell of former lives of Gautama Buddha in which he demonstrated mastery of a specific virtue or made noble choices that propelled him along the path to Buddhahood. Reading and pondering these stories and those of other great masters helps us determine what to do in a similar circumstance.

4. **"To realise the Thought of Enlightenment, to practise all the duties of a bodhisattva, to acquire all the paramitas and purify all the stages of his career."** The Buddha outlines two ways of life: random living and intentional living. Intentional living takes self-discipline, striving, and the exercise of our faculties. It takes practice, and practice makes perfect. Through living with intention and through patient and steadfast practice, we are remade and we forge our God-identity.

5. **"To mature all beings and establish them in the knowledge of the Buddha, [namely,] all the four classes of beings who are in the six states of existence."** The four classes of beings are classifications of individuals according to the ease or difficulty with which they can understand and embrace the teachings. The six states

of existence refer literally to states that range from the celestial realm to the hell-regions and figuratively to various states of consciousness that range from high to low.

Not all souls can be reached through the same approach or with the same teaching. As bodhisattvas, we devote ourselves to finding various and creative means to reach different types of people. And to ensure passing the teachings on to future generations, we give light and enlightenment to the children.

6. **"To perceive the whole universe."** As we progress on our path, we begin to perceive the oneness of all life. We begin to perceive that God and all beings are contained within the universe and also contain it. This is what is meant by cosmic consciousness. It's an awareness that goes far beyond provincialism, narrow-mindedness, fanaticism, the belief that nobody's right except the people who are just like us, et cetera.

When we embody cosmic consciousness, it will leaven the whole planet. We will see people liberated from centuries-old narrowness of thought and concepts. They will be liberated to also perceive the whole universe and everything in it as God and to transmute that which has been misqualified in it and is not God.

7. **"To purify and cleanse all the Buddha-fields."** Buddha-fields are spiritual realms established by and presided

over by a Buddha where conditions are ideally suited to the attainment of enlightenment. As we purify and cleanse our inner world—our thoughts, feelings, psychology, all levels of our consciousness—we are preparing a fitting home for the Buddha inside of us, the seed of Buddhahood in our heart. As we clear, purify and cleanse our outer world—our body temple, home, work space, environment—we are preparing a home fit for the Buddha to manifest.

8. **"To enter on the Great Way and to produce a common thought and purpose in all bodhisattvas."** The Great Way is the Mahayana, a path that leads to universal enlightenment. When we have a one-pointed purpose and common thought that we share with others, all our energy goes toward making that happen. Through the ingenuity of the divine spark within, we devise ways to reach out to people with the teachings and to cultivate and nurture the seed of Buddhahood in them in anticipation of that moment when the thought of enlightenment, bodhicitta, arises in them.

9. **"To make all actions of the body, speech and mind fruitful and successful."** When our thoughts, actions and words are harmonious and positive, they bear good fruit and lead to success. When they come from the heart, our attitude and consciousness remain positive.

Fruitfulness and successfulness are born of the

right-mindedness that we experience after concluding our devotions. When we make contact with God and feel the light descend, we can lock in that heightened level of consciousness through our prayers and invocations.

We sustain a certain momentum of that light in our daily service. And we fortify ourselves and renew that level of consciousness each time we pray and commune with God. There is no limit to the heights of our attainment. And what we attain now is what we will take with us when our soul departs the body temple.

10. **"To attain the supreme and perfect Enlightenment and to preach the Doctrine."** Preaching the doctrine is living the doctrine. If we have not lived it, if we have not savored, chewed, digested and assimilated it, if we have not become all of it, then how will we teach it? There's nothing more joyous than to be free of the old human self with all its human nonsense and to literally be in the divine Self because we are savoring and living the doctrine.

### SEEK AND FIND THE CHILDREN

The way to ensure that the teachings are passed on to future generations is to teach the children. We have a responsibility to establish in our children their self-knowledge in God, to teach them the basic precepts for living given to us by Gautama Buddha (which in principle are the same as those given by Jesus Christ and others), to give them a basic understanding of the law of karma, and to provide them the knowledge of how to contact God and receive his response. If we give children a solid foundation in spiritual law when they are young, that understanding will remain with them and they will be able to pick up the threads of it sometime, somewhere, when they feel the inner prompting.

The desire for the path comes from within. We cannot create it. We can't make a child do what we want him or her to do. But we can prepare the soil, water and fertilize it, and plant a child's roots deeply in that soil.

We can bring the right amount of sun and love and nourishment and all things together, but that child still has free will. Still, if we have taught our children well, we will have planted in their hearts and in their souls all that they need. And all these things will be there and will ripen and unfold at that special moment when the soul needs them.

In the spirit of the bodhisattva ideal, I would ask you to seek and find the children. Give them the light and the enlightenment they need.

### AN EXTRAORDINARY DISCOURSE

Before we move on to the next illustrative vows, which are from Shantideva's *Bodhicharyavatara*, we'll look at the legend of how Shantideva came to deliver his profound discourse on the bodhisattva's way of life.

In the eighth century the monk now known as Shantideva is said to have attended the prestigious Nalanda University for a time. Some say he showed up "out of nowhere."
Outwardly this monk displayed no mastery at all; in fact, he
appeared to spend all his time either eating in the dining hall
or sleeping in the courtyard. A number of students took to
calling him Lazybones. They thought he was a disgrace to
the school and eventually they devised a plan to have him
expelled. This version of the story is attributed to Tibetan
Buddhist lama and teacher Drikung Ontul Rinpoche:

> *One day, on a special occasion during which members of
> the region's various monasteries gathered together, they
> ridiculed [Lazybones] by inviting him to give a teaching.
> They were surprised when he agreed, so to take the joke a
> bit further, they built a throne especially for him. Natu-
> rally they hoped that when the day arrived, everyone from
> miles around would have a fine time watching this person
> make a real fool of himself.*
>
> *When everyone had settled down for the talk, Lazy-
> bones climbing to his high seat, turned and asked whether
> the congregation would prefer an ordinary or an extraor-
> dinary discourse. The monks were absolutely delighted
> at that, and responded, "Oh, an extraordinary one, of
> course!"*
>
> *Then the one known to us now as Shantideva (Divine
> Peace) recited…the discourse known as the Way of the
> Bodhisattva.*

*The company was dumbstruck for, it is said, at the*
*end, Shantideva actually rose to the sky on a rainbow.*

## SHANTIDEVA'S ASPIRATION

Shantideva's bodhisattva aspiration is in the form of
a prayer. Indian scholar Har Dayal described it as "a magnificent Canticle of love and charity" that "reveals the spirit
that should animate and inspire the novice, who would
become a *bodhisattva.*"[2] This translation is by Geshe Gyatso
and Neil Elliot:

> *[T]hrough the merit I have collected...*
> *May the suffering of every living being*
> *Be brought completely to an end;*
>
> *And until all those who are sick*
> *Have been cured of their illness,*
> *May I become their medicine,*
> *Their doctor, and their nurse.*
>
> *May a rain of food and drink descend*
> *To dispel the miseries of hunger and thirst;*
> *And during the great aeon of famine,*
> *May I become their food and drink.*
>
> *May I become an inexhaustible treasury*
> *For the poor and destitute.*
> *May I be everything they might need,*
> *Placed freely at their disposal....*

*Through giving all, I shall attain the nirvana of a Buddha*
*And my bodhichitta wishes will be fulfilled.*
*I give up everything for the sake of living beings,*
*Who are the supreme objects of giving....*

*Therefore, in whatever I do,*
*I will never cause harm to others;*
*And whenever anyone encounters me,*
*May it never be meaningless for them....*

*May all those who harm me...*
*Thereby create the cause to attain enlightenment....*

*To benefit all living beings,*
*May I become a treasury of wealth,*
*Powerful mantras, potent medicine,*
*A wish-fulfilling tree, and a wish-granting cow.*

*Just like the great elements such as earth,*
*And like eternal space,*
*May I become the basis from which everything arises*
*For sustaining the life of countless living beings;*

*And, until they have passed beyond sorrow,*
*May I sustain all forms of life*
*Throughout the realms of living beings*
*That reach to the ends of space.*[3]

### THE DESIRE TO GIVE ALL

In this prayer Shantideva gives voice to the devotees of all the mystical paths of the world's religions who so love God in his creatures that they desire to give away everything they have, including themselves.

To give up everything for nirvana, we should have to draw a zero where we are standing. But the zero is really the circle of God. Giving up everything means giving up everything that is not God or of God. Our understanding of being all things to all people is the understanding that God in us can meet the needs of all whom we meet. Sometimes we may not think so, but try affirming that and see what happens.

The concept of praying for the enlightenment of all who harm us or have appeared to be our enemies is enlightened self-interest, because if our so-called enemies become enlightened they will no longer attack us. It is the best prayer to make for them.

### FINDING BALANCE THROUGH THE MIDDLE WAY

Some Buddhist texts seem to lack an awareness of the human condition; at times they may describe a level that seems beyond our ability to attain. Remember that there is a balancing factor to all things. God doesn't expect us to live in a mud hut with nothing, not even utensils for cooking food. God realizes the necessities of life. Gautama Buddha, in his first sermon following enlightenment, preached the Middle Way to his disciples *(bhikkhus)*:

*There are two extremes, O bhikkhus, which the man who
has given up the world ought not to follow—the habitual
practice, on the one hand, of self-indulgence which is un-
worthy, vain and fit only for the worldly-minded—and the
habitual practice, on the other hand, of self-mortification,
which is painful, useless and unprofitable.*

*Neither abstinence from fish or flesh, nor going naked,
nor shaving the head, nor wearing matted hair, nor dress-
ing in a rough garment, nor covering oneself with dirt, nor
sacrificing to Agni [a Vedic divinity], will cleanse a man
who is not free from delusions.*[4]

When we are free from delusions we may or may not
choose to engage in those practices. They are helpful but
symbolic, and if they are a mere covering and we are still
full of "dead men's bones"[5] then they avail nothing and
only convince us that we are getting somewhere when we
are not.

## CONCENTRATING ON WHO WE ARE

The things we cannot give away are the things with
which we identify ourselves. In other words, without these
things we would not feel that we had an identity. So rather
than concentrate on what we are giving away, let us concentrate on who we are. When we realize a greater portion
of the identity of God in us, we will see that we are able to
part easily with those things that are simply props for our
lesser consciousness.

## *Reflection on the Essence*

- Consider how your consciousness has evolved over the years and how your self-expression has shifted as a result of these changes.

- In what way might you cultivate a greater level of God-realization? Consider trying this for a period of time and see how it affects your relationship with life.

# The Buddha Replies to the Deva

On a certain day when the Blessed One [Gautama Buddha] dwelt at Jetavana, the garden of Anāthapindika, a celestial deva came to him in the shape of a Brahman whose countenance was bright and whose garments were white like snow. The deva asked questions which the Blessed One answered.

The deva said: "What is the sharpest sword? What is the deadliest poison? What is the fiercest fire? What is the darkest night?"

The Blessed One replied: "A word spoken in wrath is the sharpest sword; covetousness is the deadliest poison; passion is the fiercest fire; ignorance is the darkest night."

The deva said: "Who gains the greatest benefit? Who loses most? Which armor is invulnerable? What is the best weapon?"

The Blessed One replied: "He is the greatest gainer who gives to others, and he loses most who greedily receives without gratitude. Patience is an invulnerable armor; wisdom is the best weapon."...

The deva asked: "What causes ruin in the world? What breaks off friendships? What is the most violent fever? Who is the best physician?"

The Blessed One replied: "Ignorance causes the ruin of the world. Envy and selfishness break off friendships. Hatred is the most violent fever, and the Buddha is the best physician."[1]

# Ten Stages to Becoming a Buddha

Numerous Buddhist writings outline various stages of the bodhisattva path. These stages of spiritual progress, called bhumis, vary from text to text and from commentator to commentator, but in each case the bodhisattva strives to progress from one stage to the next until he realizes complete enlightenment.

We will be studying these stages as outlined in the Dashabhumika (Ten Stages) Sutra, which is considered to be the standard treatise on the subject. The Dashabhumika describes ten stages of spiritual progress from the bodhisattva's first cherished thought of enlightenment to his realization of supreme enlightenment and Buddhahood.

At each stage the bodhisattva practices the highest possible development of a perfection, or transcendental virtue (called a paramita). A paramita is a virtue that is perfected to a level beyond any limit. Although the bodhisattva concentrates on one perfection in each stage, he is simultaneously practicing all ten.

# 7

*First Bhumi: Pramudita*
*Joyful Stage*

The first bhumi is *Pramudita*, the Joyful Stage. The bodhisattva enters this stage upon the awakening of bodhicitta and taking the bodhisattva vow. He is deeply committed to becoming a Buddha in order to help everyone who has recourse to him. As he begins the path to Buddhahood, he experiences the joy of unlimited possibilities. He rejoices in thoughts of the Buddha and the Buddha's teaching. He recognizes the emptiness of the ego and feels the awakening of a great heart of compassion.

## DANA-PARAMITA: THE PERFECTION OF GIVING

At this stage the bodhisattva devotes himself to the perfection of Giving *(Dana)*, the first paramita. True giving is done with respect for the recipient and without hope of reward. Many Buddhists in Asian countries look for an opportunity each day to give something, even if all they can give is a few spoonfuls of rice. There is such a sense of freedom in simply giving.

Buddhists teach that giving is threefold: the giving of material goods, the giving of fearlessness, and the giving of the dharma (the teaching). Another important aspect of giving is known as the transference of merit. The bodhisattva willingly gives all his acquired merit for the salvation of all beings.

In *Quietly Comes the Buddha*, Gautama Buddha describes the perfection of giving as "the total giving of oneself, the continual emptying of the jar of water, that the jar might be filled again."[1] The same idea is expressed in a short sutra on giving that records Gautama as having said, "If the living beings knew the fruit and final reward of charity and the distribution of gifts, as I know them, then they would not eat their food without giving to others and sharing with others, even if it were their last morsel and mouthful."[2]

I am reminded of the Old Testament saying, "Cast thy bread upon the waters, for thou shalt find it after many days"[3]—after many days it will return to you. What we freely give reaches to the farthest edge of the cosmos, then turns around and comes back, bringing to our shore, multiplied, what we have sent out.

## PRINCE VISHVANTARA GIVES ALL

The story of Prince Vishvantara is a supreme example of one who practiced the perfection of giving. This is one of the hundreds of stories called the jataka tales, "birth stories" that relate how Gautama in previous embodiments fulfilled each of the requirements of the bodhisattva path.

*Vishvantara was a prince, and from the moment of his birth his generosity was noted by the gods. With his first breath he miraculously spoke out: "Mother, I will give a gift. What gift shall I make?" At age eight, inspired by a desire to give something that was his very own, he declared, "If someone asks me to give him my heart or my eyes or my flesh, I will do it." The gods again took note. The skies roared and the earth shook.*

*As Vishvantara grew older, news of his generosity spread far and wide. He gave alms regularly, often while riding the royal white elephant, a truly magnificent creature. Many came to associate this white elephant with the kingdom's prosperity and abundant harvests.*

*One day while Prince Vishvantara was distributing alms, the emissaries of a neighboring country asked him for the white elephant in hopes of relieving their country's severe drought. Vishvantara graciously consented. This act sparked such an outcry against him that his father, the king, had no choice but to exile him. Vishvantara spent his last day in the kingdom giving away all his possessions.*

*The next morning Vishvantara set out from the king-dom accompanied by his devoted wife, Madri, and their two children. They began their journey in a chariot drawn by four horses. Soon they met some priests who asked for the horses and another who asked for the chariot. Vishvantara willingly gave them away and the family continued on foot to their destination. They lived in simple huts made from local vegetation and they ate wild roots and fruits.*

*One day while Madri was away an elderly brahmin came and asked Vishvantara to give him the children as servants for his wife. Vishvantara agreed. Though he felt agony in parting with them, he nonetheless rejoiced at the opportunity to give what was so dear to him. Madri was brokenhearted.*

*Then Shakra, the king of the gods, appeared to Vishvantara disguised as a poor priest and asked him for his cherished Madri. Vishvantara consented. Understanding her husband's pure motive, Madri silently submitted.*

*In that moment the heavens trembled and the oceans roared their approval. The gods acknowledged that Vishvantara had achieved perfect knowledge and had demonstrated perfect charity. Shakra resumed his own form, blessed Vishvantara and returned Madri to him.*

*A short while later the two children, who had been ransomed by their grandfather the king, were returned to Prince Vishvantara and Madri. The king and his subjects, deeply moved by Vishvantara's selflessness, recalled him from exile and gloriously reinstated him.*

*According to Buddhist tradition, Vishvantara was reborn in his next life as Gautama Buddha.*

## Reflection on the Essence

• What does true giving mean to you?

• In what practical ways do you express joyful giving in your life?

• What feelings do genuine giving evoke for you?

**Siddhartha Gautama as a Bodhisattva-Prince.**
*This statue depicts Gautama as a nobleman of
the Sakya clan, before he became a Buddha.
The* prabha *(halo, symbolizing the light
emanating from him) and draped garment
indicate his bodhisattva status.*

# 8

## Second Bhumi: Vimala
## Immaculate Stage

The second bhumi is *Vimala,* Immaculate Stage. The bodhisattva attains to this stage by purity of conduct. He is incorruptible, free from desire, and has developed true self-control. He is forthright with himself and others, free of any evasiveness or ambiguity. He is calm yet active and is tenderhearted, beneficent, noble and magnanimous toward all.

### *SILA-PARAMITA:* THE PERFECTION OF MORALITY

At this stage the bodhisattva devotes special attention to the perfection of Morality *(Sila),* the second paramita. He lives an exemplary life of purity and meritorious action. He resolves to be the friend, guide, protector, teacher and saviour of others.

By his example and teaching, the bodhisattva inspires

and encourages others to follow the Ten Precepts. This means abstaining from sins of body, speech and mind. Traditionally, these are: killing (which includes taking life in any form), stealing, sexual misconduct, lying, slander, coarse, abusive or insulting language, frivolous speech (empty chatter and gossip), covetousness (greedy desire), malice and angry speech, and false views (delusion).

Sangharakshita writes, "To however great an extent the Bodhisattva practises the Perfection of Morality he will never think of himself as virtuous…. He will wear his righteousness as lightly as a flower."[1]

Concepts of what is moral and what is immoral differ according to religious and ethnic customs and times. From the standpoint of the spiritual path, moral and immoral practices can be defined as those that either enhance or detract from the goal of union with God. Whatever gets us closer to God by legitimate means is good. Whatever puts us further away from God is not good.

## THE NOBLE EIGHTFOLD PATH

The Buddha taught that morality is the foundation for a single-pointed mind and that the practice of morality is the perfect method for protecting the mind from the influence of delusions. For this reason he set forth a moral code in his Noble Eightfold Path, which consists of eight precepts for right living. These are listed with my understanding of how we cultivate them.

Right Understanding (or Right Views) comes from attunement to the will of God.

Right Aspiration (or Right Thought) comes with the purification and illumination of the crown chakra and mind.

Right Speech comes as divine love flows from the heart, allowing and inspiring speech that uplifts life.

Right Action comes when our motive is pure, and purity of motive leads to honorable behavior.

Right Livelihood comes from being centered in the truth, living honorably and engaging only in occupations that uplift.

Right Effort comes from compassionate caring and involves service and ministration to one another and to all life.

Right Mindfulness comes when our motive is to wed our free will to God's will and when our desire is to attain and lead others to soul liberation.

Right Concentration (or Right Absorption) comes as we attain integration through the heart.

In summary, when we practice harmlessness *(ahimsa)* and do all to the glory of God, then our thoughts, speech and actions will be right and we will have the full reward.

## THE CHAPLAIN OF GREAT MORALITY

One of the jataka tales tells of a lifetime in which Gautama was embodied as a king's chaplain. In this tale the chaplain, a man of great morality, makes a test of the virtue in order to deepen his understanding.

*A king's chaplain demonstrated great morality and was respected by all. The king in particular accorded him exceptional respect. This special treatment eventually caused him to think, "Does the king honor me with superior respect because of my birth, my family or my position? Is it because of the talents I have? Or could this special treatment by the king be due to the morality I have acquired? I shall put this to a test."*

*So then he decided what he would do. And on three consecutive days, allowing his actions to be seen, he stole gold coins to see how the people would react. On the first two days, out of respect for him, those who had observed the thefts said nothing. Finally, on the third day, they denounced him as a thief.*

*People gathered at the scene, bound him and took him to the king. Speaking sternly to the chaplain, the king asked, "How has it come to pass that you have committed this highly immoral act?" Then the king commanded that his order regarding this criminal be carried out.*

*The chaplain explained his motive to the king and said, "From the order you have just given, I now know that your respectful treatment of me was due to my morality and not to my birth, family, race or position. Morality is chief among blessings. Nothing in this world is esteemed higher than morality. I shall devote myself to perfecting morality. Allow me to leave here to become a hermit."*

*The king granted the chaplain's request. The chaplain retired from the world in order to practice morality in its entirety and he eventually became an arhat (worthy one).*

## THE STUDENT WHO REFUSED TO STEAL

A later jataka tale tells of a somewhat later embodiment of Gautama, who by then had become a bodhisattva. He was studying under an illustrious teacher who decided to put his students' virtue to the test. In this tale, the bodhisattva's understanding of morality is more refined than that of the chaplain in the preceding tale, illustrating the point that we bring into succeeding embodiments the lessons we learn along the way.

*The bodhisattva's teacher decided to test the virtue of his students. He explained to them that he intended to give his daughter in marriage but that she must first have the proper attire. The teacher invited the students to steal dresses and ornaments for her, cautioning them that he would accept only what no one had seen them take and that he would refuse anything they had allowed to be seen.*

*Out of the class of five hundred students, only the bodhisattva refused to steal. When the teacher asked why he had refused, the bodhisattva replied that there is no such thing as secrecy in wrongdoing.*

*The teacher then explained that his motive in requesting that the students steal had been to test them in* order to find a truly virtuous man for his daughter. He instructed the students to return all that they had taken and told the bodhisattva that he alone had proved worthy of his daughter. The teacher then adorned his daughter from his own wealth and gave her in marriage to the bodhisattva.

## Reflection on the Essence

- Reflect on a time when you faced a difficult moral decision. What considerations led you to the decision you made in that instance?

- What did you learn from that situation?

- In what practical ways can your understanding of morality be applied to improve your life and that of others?

# 9

# Third Bhumi: Prabhakari
# Illuminating Stage

The third bhumi is *Prabhakari,* Illuminating Stage. At this stage the bodhisattva's mind radiates the light of the doctrine. He realizes that a material body, subject as it is to suffering, pain and grief, burns with the fire of passion, hatred and error. He therefore cultivates indifference to the impermanent things of the world.

The bodhisattva yearns intensely for enlightenment and truth. He renews his determination to assist, guide and liberate all beings. In his striving for Buddha-knowledge, he diligently devotes himself to the study of the sutras and other teachings of the Buddha. He engages in profound meditation and introspection and roots out all imperfections.

### KSANTI-PARAMITA: THE PERFECTION OF PATIENCE

The bodhisattva at this stage cultivates the perfection of Patience *(Ksanti),* the third paramita. Ksanti is also translated as forgiveness, forbearance or endurance, and it encompasses gentleness and true humility.

According to Buddhist teachings, there are three aspects of patience: the patience of forgiveness, the patience of being able to accept suffering, and the patience of being able to engage in virtuous practice. Geshe Gyatso teaches that the perfection of patience

> ... *concerns the way we react to the beings and objects that harm us. We must realize that there is no way for us to overcome all our external foes. If we defeat one enemy, another always arises to take his place. If we kill someone who has harmed us, his relatives and friends will attack us in revenge. How is it possible... to be free from all enemies who are as infinite as the expanse of space? Only by defeating our own anger can we overcome those who would harm us.*[1]

Rather than reacting in anger, a bodhisattva always forgives. He forgives others for every injury and abuse. Dayal described it this way: "He forgives them everywhere, in secret and in public."[2]

## THE ANATOMY OF FORGIVENESS

It can be a very hard thing to forgive certain acts taken by people. It can be hard to forgive a child molester who has taken something of the soul of a child that may not be regained in that life. It can be hard to forgive the murderer, the rapist, the one who sets fire to a house or destroys a business, and so forth. So what is the anatomy of forgiveness that we can truly follow in good conscience and with profound sincerity and no withholding?

First we look at the anatomy of the individual. An individual is composed of many parts: a divine spark, a soul that has the potential to become God, an inner God Presence, and four lower bodies (etheric, mental, emotional and physical). The individual contains a complete record of all that has transpired, positive and negative, since his soul first embodied—the record of all karma, the psychology of the unconscious and subconscious, and all positive momentums as well as those that are not of the light, such as greed, avarice, murderous intent, and so on.

Among these components, who or what is it that commits the act? It is the soul that somehow has gotten entangled and overtaken by the "not-self." We have created this not-self over the course of many lifetimes, beginning with the very first moment when we cast doubt upon God or upon his sons and daughters. So, caught between the not-self and the reasoning conscious mind, the soul is at times swayed to perform certain actions that are not of the light.

### THE POTENTIAL TO REALIZE GOD

The soul may be tainted and impure and have all kinds of problems, but that soul still has the potential to one day realize God. Therefore, no matter how bad an action or crime may be, we can still call on the law of forgiveness for that soul. We can pray for the soul to be taught by God on inner levels and to be liberated from momentums of a wounded psychology and from records of the past that have caused that soul to make the decision to sin. We can give violet-flame mantras, such as those in chapter 18. And we can call to God for forgiveness and pray for that soul to make a turnaround and to come into the service of God.

### FINDING FREEDOM THROUGH INNER WORK

It is not necessary to communicate with the person we are praying for. We simply do our inner work, offering our prayers, striving to call forth even more mercy and justice and assistance than may be necessary to balance a situation, and then we leave the rest to God. And when our inner work is done, we can know with absolute certainty that in God's own perfect time and way justice will be meted out, the soul will be assisted, and if opportunity is forthcoming it will be given. This gives us a sense of having fulfilled the higher law.

By truly placing everything in God's hands, we can free ourselves and others from anger, resentment, hatred, a desire for revenge. Harboring feelings such as these could

set a soul on a dangerous course, both in this life and beyond, and it's not necessary. We can get over these things.
And if we have made karma along the way, then we can come
out knowing that we have walked the last mile in service to
balance that karma.

Practicing this forgiveness exercise—invoking the spiritual law of God and making total peace with the situation—
helps to liberate both us and others from elements of consciousness that are not right. We pray for ourselves and the
other person to be free and to be enlightened. We pray for
their soul and our own to be repolarized to the Presence of
God, the soul united with the heart and the purified mind.
And we ask that our prayers be multiplied to assist all people
who are in a similar situation. In this way we give joyously
and liberally to all, giving to them in the way that is best
for them.

## ENDURING OUR KARMA

Ksanti as the perfection of patience and endurance also
involves enduring our karma. Until we have balanced 100
percent of our karma, we will have karma to endure. Now,
the situations we face can be karmic or the testing of our
soul or a temptation that we need to run away from. If we
are unsure which of these a particular situation is, we can
pray about it and give ourselves to God. And if we need it,
we can seek counsel.

Enduring our karma is such a necessity on the Path.

The saints and bodhisattvas—which includes you and me becoming saints, you and me becoming bodhisattvas—learn to draw into the fiery vortex of the heart the energies of both personal and planetary karma that require transmutation.

## THE BUDDHA'S SERMON ON ABUSE

Jesus told his disciples, "In your patience possess ye your souls."³ The Buddha taught this same principle. This next jataka tale illustrates the perfection of ksanti.

*A foolish man learning that the Buddha observed the principle of great love which commends the return of good for evil, came and abused him. The Buddha was silent, pitying his folly.*

*When the man had finished his abuse, the Buddha asked him, saying: "Son, if a man declined to accept a present made to him, to whom would it belong?" And he answered: "In that case it would belong to the man who offered it."*

*"My son," said the Buddha, "thou hast railed at me, but I decline to accept thy abuse, and request thee to keep it thyself….*

*"A wicked man who reproaches a virtuous one is like one who looks up and spits at heaven; the spittle soils not the heaven, but comes back and defiles his own person.*

*"The slanderer is like one who flings dust at another when the wind is contrary; the dust does but return on*

*him who threw it. The virtuous man cannot be hurt and the misery that the other would inflict comes back on himself.*"[4]

## Reflection on the Essence

- *In what ways could acting with patience, forbearance and endurance improve your joy and well-being?*

## Meditation on Illumination

*This meditation is for expanding wisdom and radiating the flame of illumination to bless all life.*

Close your eyes and pour your love and gratitude to God. The love you send to God in this moment will return to you as his wisdom.

Visualize the blazing fire of illumination's flame at the point of the crown. Lightly touch the crown of your head with the fingers of your left hand. Cup your right hand in your lap in a receptive mode.

See your head and crown chakra surrounded by and infused with the golden-yellow light of illumination. Visualize the Buddha superimposed over your body and feel or imagine that your entire being is illuminated with every breath you take.

See the light going forth in all directions for the blessing of life. Imagine that light dissolving anything that is not like it until all becomes light. If you wish, you can meditate on these words:

> *O flame of light bright and gold,*
> *O flame most wondrous to behold,*
> *I am in every brain cell shining,*
> *I am in light's wisdom all divining.*
> *Ceaseless, flowing fount*
> *of illumination flaming,*
> *I am, I am, I am illumination.*

# 10

## Fourth Bhumi: Arcismati
## Radiant Stage

The fourth bhumi is *Arcismati,* Radiant (or Blazing) Stage. Although the bodhisattva has attained great spiritual heights in the first three stages, it is at this fourth stage that his attachment to self comes to a complete end.

In this stage the bodhisattva burns up sin and ignorance and enters into the light of the doctrine. He radiates energy in the same way that the sun radiates heat and light. According to an ancient text, in this stage the bodhisattva is "possessed of the blazing fire of knowledge by which all the defiling elements that resemble fuel are consumed."[1]

This need not be a future happening. We can do this right now by burning up sin and ignorance in the violet flame and by entering into the light of the Buddha and the doctrine. And we *are* radiating energy just as the sun is radiating heat and light.

## *VIRYA-PARAMITA:* THE PERFECTION OF VIGOR

In this stage the bodhisattva practices the perfection of Vigor or Energy *(Virya),* the fourth paramita. Dayal wrote: "Enlightenment depends entirely on *vīrya*…. It is far better to live only for a day with full *vīrya* than to vegetate without energy during a hundred years."[2]

Virya is the energy and zeal necessary to overcome faults, develop virtue, study the teachings, and serve others. Yes, these do take physical strength. When we don't have physical strength, our mind is not strong, our will is not strong. Virya unites us to that which is excellent and is generally defined as "energy in the pursuit of the Good."[3]

We can each determine for ourselves how we can best acquire virya through exercise, diet, lifestyle choices, and so forth, so that we can live and deliver the teachings with virya and the authority of our God Presence and Inner Buddha. When we do this, we will see how people will believe and be led to the path because they will recognize God speaking through us.

### WARRIORS OF THE SPIRIT

Some saints and exceptionally determined individuals have overcome enormous adversities, infirmities and weaknesses of the body and have accomplished far more than the vast majority of mankind who had perfect health and all the things in life that they wanted. If we could see and know what some have achieved by the will of the spirit, we would understand that there is nothing in this octave that can stop a warrior who has this true spirit. This, too, is a definition of virya.

Virya can be understood as the fire of the heart that we develop through fixed and pointed meditation upon the Buddha's heart of fire. We develop it by cultivating deep feelings of God and of God in manifestation, and through expressing gratitude for all that God has done for us. This gratitude is a profound love, a love that is a profound joy. The fire of love increases and increases through this divine interchange. This is love that will lay down a portion of the self so that another might see, another might know, another might be more of the living fire of God.

## HOLDING TO THE GOAL IN THE FACE OF HARDSHIP

A person of virya, when faced with hardship and difficulties, never falters. He holds to his goals with zeal and courage even in the face of death. Gautama demonstrated virya through his resolute determination to realize supreme enlightenment. Zen Buddhists often ponder these words that Gautama is said to have spoken while sitting beneath the Bo tree on the eve of his enlightenment: "Though only my skin, sinews and bones remain, and my blood and flesh dry up and wither away, yet will I never stir from this seat until I have attained full enlightenment."

## JANAKA ACHIEVES PERFECT VIRYA

The ancient tale of Janaka tells of a past embodiment of Gautama Buddha as a bodhisattva who achieved perfect virya.

*The Blessed One [Gautama Buddha] in a previous life was born as Janaka, a prosperous merchant who sailed the oceans in search of wealth. On one occasion his ship was wrecked in mid-ocean. Some of the crew braved the waters and perished. Others stayed aboard the ship, imploring the gods to save them, and these too died. Janaka alone, in his absolute determination to survive, smeared his body with oil, climbed to the top of the mast, and jumped far out into the sea beyond reach of the hungry fish that had gathered close to the ship.*

*For seven full days, though no land was in sight, Janaka swam courageously, unflinchingly. At mid-day on the eighth day, a deva appeared and offered him food. As it was Janaka's spiritual practice to fast from mid-day on, he graciously declined the deva's offering.*

*Then the deva tested Janaka again, saying he was a fool to keep swimming without any sign of land. Janaka replied that though he might fail, there was no disgrace in striving to reach his goal; disgrace would only befall him if, through laziness, he should make no effort. The goddess was pleased with Janaka's mastery of virya as demonstrated by his bold perseverance in the face of extreme difficulty. She led him safely to shore.*

### ONE MAN'S VIRYA SAVES MANY LIVES

Eddie Rickenbacker was a famous World War I fighter pilot and an aviation transport pioneer. Summarized here from his 1967 autobiography are two remarkable incidents in which he demonstrated virya:

> *Early in 1941, the airplane on which Rickenbacker was traveling crashed. He was pinned in the wreckage and his body lay soaking in spilled fuel. Though he suffered head injuries, crushed nerves and multiple shattered or broken bones, Rickenbacker remained conscious and provided solace and encouragement to those around him who had also survived the crash. He directed those who were able to walk to go in search of help.*
>
> *In his autobiography, Rickenbacker tells that during the rescue on the following day, though he was conscious and in tremendous pain, the ambulance personnel somehow overlooked him for a time while they removed bodies of the dead. Later, at the hospital, he was again left unattended for a time as his doctors and staff cared for "the live ones."*
>
> *Rickenbacker's injuries were extreme. For ten days he hovered near death and he remained hospitalized for several months. Even then he was not fully recovered. In his autobiography, he spoke of the supreme act of will that had been necessary to stave off death. Through it all he never gave up his resolve to live.*

~   ~   ~

*In 1942, just twenty months after that plane crash, Rickenbacker again came close to death. World War II was underway and Rickenbacker was working as a consultant for the military. While flying on a secret mission, his plane went off course and the pilots made an emergency landing in the Pacific Ocean. Rickenbacker and the others drifted at sea for twenty-four days, suffering from exposure, dehydration and starvation before being rescued. Through remarkable circumstances, all but one survived.*

    *After the first three days of drifting, their food ran out. They lived on water from the occasional rainfall until the eighth day. On that day a seagull landed on Rickenbacker's head. Moving ever so carefully and slowly, he captured the bird and shared the meal equally among all, saving some bits to use as fishing bait. During those twenty-four days, Rickenbacker led the group, encouraging them to persevere and instilling them with the spirit and will to live.*

## Reflection on the Essence

- *Recall a time when you displayed virya by persevering in a challenging situation. What motivated you to keep moving toward your goal?*

- *What inspiration do you find in the stories that reflect the essence of* virya *as energy, vigor, or perseverance?*

- *Is there one small step you might commit to today to increase your virya?*

# 11

## Fifth Bhumi: Sudurjaya
## Very-Difficult-to-Conquer Stage

The fifth bhumi is *Sudurjaya*, Very-Difficult-to-Conquer Stage. It is said that at this stage the bodhisattva is unable to be conquered by the forces of evil. He further develops purity and equanimity and truly comprehends the Four Noble Truths:

First, that life is suffering *(dukkha)*.

Second, that the cause of suffering is desire.

Third, that there is freedom or cessation from suffering through the attainment of liberation (nirvana).

And fourth, that the way to this liberation is through the Noble Eightfold Path.

Every time we desire something and can't have it, we suffer. That's the great conclusion of Gautama Buddha— that life is suffering and the root of that suffering is that we all have desires.

At this stage the bodhisattva pities the people of the world who are the slaves of pride and desire, and he devotes himself further to their liberation. Out of compassion he seeks to meet the needs of the world in which he lives. He acquires knowledge of the arts and sciences, accelerating in a field through which he can give to others and teach them.

Sangharakshita points out that wherever Buddhism spread in Asia it was a carrier of culture, the arts, science and knowledge of all kinds, and not just of religious doctrines, teachings and practices. As he puts it, "through the arts, through the sciences, the mind and the heart—the intelligence, the emotions—these are refined [and] become more closely attuned to spiritual things."[1]

Some commentators apply the label "difficult to conquer" to the stage itself, saying that as long as the bodhisattva still despairs at the state of the world, he remains at this stage. The twelfth-century Tibetan Buddhist teacher sGam.po.pa, Milarepa's foremost student, explained it this way: "On this level there are two difficulties: (i) striving to bring sentient beings to spiritual maturity while (ii) not becoming emotionally unstable when they make a mess of everything done for them."[2]

### DHYANA-PARAMITA: THE PERFECTION OF MEDITATION

In this stage the bodhisattva concentrates on the perfection of Meditation or Concentration (*Dhyana*), the fifth paramita. All schools of Buddhism agree that for the safe and fruitful practice of meditation a period of retirement from the world is necessary. This period can be long or short depending on the disciple's progress.

Buddhists teach that wisdom arises from the single-pointed mind. They use the analogy of a candle. When a candle is placed where there is no draft, it illumines the entire room. Likewise, when the mind is clear and still, free from distraction, clear insight results.

In the classical Tibetan text *The Jewel Ornament of Liberation,* sGam.po.pa stated: "He who does not practise meditation, though he...possess all other qualities, falls into the power of restlessness and his mind is wounded by the fangs of conflicting emotions."[3]

### A CORD OF LIVING FLAME

A heart and mind stayed upon God creates a strong cord of living flame. Those who experience this know how much light can flow over this cord to reach many souls, and they are not able to turn to the right or the left of that goal. The cord of living flame exerts such a pull and gives such a blessing that, for those who experience it, it becomes the means to saving many, including their own soul.

### THE POWER OF A PILGRIM'S PRAYER

The power of dhyana is dramatically illustrated in a story told by a Chinese pilgrim, Hsüan-tsang, who visited India in the seventh century. While sailing on the Ganges, his boat was attacked by pirates who decided to kill him as a sacrificial offering to their god. Hsüan-tsang asked to be given a few moments to prepare to enter nirvana. What happened next is recounted by René Grousset, a French author and specialist in Asiatic and Oriental history:

> *[The pilgrim Hsüan-tsang] meditated lovingly upon the Bodhisattva Maitreya and turned all his thoughts to the Heaven of the Blessed Ones, praying ardently that he might be reborn there in order to offer his respects and pay homage to the Bodhisattva; that he might hear the most excellent Law expounded and reach perfect enlightenment (Buddha-hood); that he might then redescend and be born again on earth to teach and convert these men and bring them to perform the acts of higher virtue, to abandon their infamous beliefs; and finally that he might spread far and wide all the benefits of the Law and bring peace and happiness to all creatures. He then... sat down in a posture of contemplation and eagerly bent his thoughts upon the Bodhisattva Maitreya....*
>
> *All of a sudden... he felt himself raised up to Mount Sumeru, and after having passed through one, two and then three heavens, he saw the true Maitreya seated upon a glittering throne... surrounded by a multitude of gods.... Suddenly a furious wind sprang up all around them... beating up the waves of the river and swamping all the boats.*[4]

This caused the pirates to be terrified. Repenting, they threw themselves at Hsüan-tsang's feet.

## Reflection on the Essence

- *In what practical ways have you benefited from engaging in reflection, meditation, or concentration?*

- *What benefits might you expect in your life from taking a step toward deepening this ability?*

# How Long Does It Take to Become a Buddha?

At this point you may be wondering how long it takes to progress through all the stages to Buddhhood. Har Dayal wrote: "A bodhisattva, who has taken the Vow, has an incredibly long pilgrimage before him. He will reach his goal and become a Buddha after the lapse of a very long period of time, in comparison with which even geological and astronomical figures pale into insignificance."[1]

The Mahayana sutras tell us that the bodhisattva career takes "three countless kalpas." The Treatise on the Great Perfection of Wisdom describes the length of a kalpa as "longer than the time required to wear away a cube of stone 40 ri (one ri is about 600 meters) on each side, if a heavenly nymph alights on it and brushes it with a piece of cloth once every hundred years."[2]

In Buddhist cosmology, a kalpa is one-fourth of the duration of time from the origination to the destruction of a world system. According to the calculations of Dayal, a bodhisattva's career spans about "four times nine hundred sixty thousand

*million billion billion billion billions of years." Depending on how we define a kalpa, he says it may take "only 960 million years."*[3]

Don't despair yet! The Tantric scriptures record the Buddha as saying that Buddhahood can be achieved in sixteen lifetimes or less. And at least one Mahayana sect believes it is possible to attain Buddhahood in one lifetime. It is said that the bodhisattva Kuan Yin leapt immediately from the first to the eighth stage of the bodhisattva path.

The key we have today is the violet flame. It's the key to acceleration, and we accelerate by giving our all to this path, diligently calling forth the violet flame of forgiveness, balancing our karma with enthusiasm and joy, and passing our tests.

## CYCLES OF INCREASING MASTERY

As we study the stages of the bodhisattva path in various Buddhist texts, we find some overlap and repetition in the descriptions of the bodhisattva's attainment, consciousness and activities from one stage to the next. With each new stage, the bodhisattva enters a new level of initiation. He gains new initiations, more advanced ones, but often these are on the same principles as the preceding ones.

Cycle by cycle, the bodhisattva's mastery grows. It's like learning to play the piano. We start with a simple melody and then gradually add chords and harmonies. Eventually the melody deepens and becomes richer, and we acquire greater mastery and attainment.

*Gautama Buddha in Meditation.*
*The hands are positioned in the* bhumisparsa mudra
*(earth-touching gesture). The* usnisa *(topknot) symbolizes*
*the Buddha's spiritual sovereignty.*

# 12

*Sixth Bhumi: Abhimukhi*
*Face-to-Face Stage*

*T*he sixth bhumi is *Abhimukhi,* Face-to-Face Stage. In this stage the bodhisattva draws nigh to Reality and advances further toward Buddha-knowledge. He is free from desire and sees beyond the relative perceptions of I and Other, Doer and Knower, Existence and Nonexistence.

This bhumi is sometimes called the Proximate Stage because the bodhisattva stands "proximate to the properties of the Buddha."[1] The bodhisattva has the attainment of an arhat and could enter nirvana, freed from the rounds of death and rebirth. But out of intense compassion for all beings, he chooses to remain with the world until he can bring everyone with him. A popular Zen Buddhist story illustrates this concept.

## THREE MEN AND A WALL

*Three men are wandering in the wilderness when they come upon a walled compound. One of them boosts another one up to see what's on the other side. After surveying the scene, he goes into bliss and climbs over the wall. Then the second one is boosted up. He, too, peers over the edge and immediately climbs over, abandoning the third.*

*The third one is highly motivated to find out what's on the other side. With great difficulty he climbs to the top of the wall. On the other side he sees a paradise with lush vegetation, trees bearing ripe fruit, and a stream of crystal clear water. But instead of crossing over, he climbs back down to tell the world of his discovery.*

## *PRAJNA-PARAMITA:* THE PERFECTION OF WISDOM

At this stage the bodhisattva cultivates the perfection of Wisdom *(Prajna)*, the sixth paramita. The Great Compassion Heart Dharani Sutra records the famous vows of Kuan Yin. Among these is the bodhisattva's vow to "quickly board the prajna boat," meaning to quickly acquire wisdom. Another sutra says that prajna routs the army of Mara (the forces of temptation) as water destroys a vessel made of unbaked clay.

A bodhisattva who has acquired prajna gives away all that he has and his character is impeccable. Motivated by great love and compassion, he deepens his practice of meditation, attains greater powers of concentration, and remains unmoved by temptation.

Prajna has been called the close friend of the bodhisattva and the "pearl of great price." This is because the bodhisattva, in truly achieving the transcendental level of perfection of these virtues, practices them with prajna. Thus, prajna is considered to include all the other paramitas and is said to be greater than them all.

A number of Buddhist scriptures are devoted to the perfection of prajna. But prajna goes beyond a simple understanding of wisdom. The bodhisattva with true prajna knows Reality fully and deeply. This perfected wisdom takes the bodhisattva to a level of understanding that is beyond opposites, beyond duality.

## WISDOM AND COMPASSION IN THE BODHISATTVA

A story from the Vimalakirti Nirdesa (Spoken by Vimalakirti) Sutra illustrates the concept of wisdom that is beyond duality and also gives us a glimpse into the nature of true compassion. Vimalakirti (Spotless Reputation) is a bodhisattva from the realm of profound joy who has perfected himself in every virtue and appears on earth in the guise of a wealthy householder in order to teach certain lessons. Here he conveys a lesson on the nature of sickness:

*At a certain assembly of the Buddha, Vimalakirti was not present on account of sickness, so Buddha asked various Bodhisattvas to go to inquire after his illness, but one and*

*all declined on the ground that they were not worthy, giving*
*specific instances of his wisdom and virtue. At last Manjusri*
*undertook to go. In answer to his question as to his health,*
Vimalakirti replied in famous words: "The sickness of a
Bodhisattva comes from great compassion, and exists in
the time of ignorance which is possessed by every being.
When the sickness of every being is ended, then my sickness will also end. I am sick because beings are sick."[2]

## TRUE COMPASSION IS WITHOUT SENTIMENTALITY

The Vimalakirti Sutra conveys a sublime teaching on
the path of the bodhisattva. The bodhisattva bears the dis-
eases of the people of the earth in his body, yet he affirms
that they are not real because the body is insubstantial and
the mind is ephemeral. He does not try to get rid of these
sicknesses for the comfort of himself but bears them for the
comfort of others.

Vimalakirti says the compassion of the bodhisattva is
without sentimentality. He explains that sentimental views
exhaust an individual by reinforcing the human condition,
therefore tying the sentimental person into it. In contrast,
great compassion is free of sentimentality and is never
exhausting. Thus, the bodhisattva expresses compassion
while keeping his mind free of involvement. The bodhisattva
refuses to lock gears with the karma of a person. Rather, he
uplifts that person to a higher dimension of his being.

If we are going to lift people up, we cannot tie into lower

emotions and passions. We cannot help others if we descend to their level. We remain at our own level and uplift them with great compassion.

*Reflection on the Essence*

- In what way(s) can you see yourself in the story of the three men and the wall?

- Recall a time when you acted with true compassion and another time when you acted with sentimentality. Compare any differences you perceive in how each of these affected you. How did they impact the person or situation you were engaged in helping?

- How does Vimalakirti's teaching on sickness illumine your understanding?

# Tibetan Prayer to Manjushri

Manjushri, the Bodhisattva of Wisdom, is a being of Buddhic attainment. Tibetan Buddhists offer a prayer to Manjushri that invokes wisdom and illumination. In this prayer, when we "bow down" to him, we are bowing to the light within him. The reference to Manjushri as the "compassionate one" underscores the perfect balance of wisdom and compassion in fully enlightened beings.

*I bow down to you, O Manjushri.*
*With the brilliance of your wisdom,*
*O compassionate one,*
*Illuminate the darkness enclosing my mind.*
*Enlighten my intelligence and wisdom*
*So that I may gain insight*
*Into Buddha's words and the texts*
*That explain them.*[1]

*Manjushri's flaming sword represents wisdom,*
*which cuts through ignorance. The flower supports the*
*Prajnaparamita Sutra, symbolizing enlightenment.*

# 13

## Seventh Bhumi: Duramgama
## Far-Reaching Stage

The seventh bhumi is *Duramgama*, Far-Reaching Stage. Commentators are reticent to speculate about what occurs on the bodhisattva path beyond the sixth stage. Beatrice Suzuki writes:

> The Bodhisattva is now a very high being indeed, so high that our ordinary, relative minds cannot follow him. To understand him now we must ourselves stand where he is....
>
> He is now skilled in all means of leading others to Bodhi. This stage...gives the full development of the intelligence of the Bodhisattva. Although he no longer has worldly thoughts he can, through his great compassion, assist others in their troubles in this world, and he turns over his merit to assist them.[1]

Sangharakshita explains: "From this point onwards all attempts to describe the Stages through which he passes must inevitably result in...misrepresentation.... The Bodhisattva's progress is no longer that of an individual. He is now an impersonal cosmic force."[2]

Scholar H. Wolfgang Schumann says that at this stage "the Bodhisattva changes over into a new mode of being. He becomes a *Transcendent* Bodhisattva, which means that he is no longer tied to a physical body."[3]

D. T. Suzuki describes it this way:

*In short, the Bodhisattva himself lives on a higher plane of spirituality far removed from the defilements of worldliness; but he does not withdraw himself to this serene, unmolested subjectivity; he boldly sets out in the world of particulars and senses; and, placing himself on the level of ignorant beings, he works like them, he toils like them, and suffers like them; and he never fails all these times to practise the gospel of lovingkindness and to turn over...all his merits towards the emancipation and spiritual edification of the masses, that is, he never gets tired of practising the ten virtues of perfection.*[4]

### UPAYA-PARAMITA: THE PERFECTION OF SKILLFUL MEANS

In this stage the bodhisattva practices all the ten paramitas, but he especially cultivates the perfection of Skillful

Means *(Upaya)*, the seventh paramita. This means he devises all possible ways to instruct and liberate souls. In the sutra that bears his name, Vimalakirti says, "Prajna is the mother of the Bodhisattva and Upaya his father; there is no leader of humanity who is not born of them."[5] While only wisdom can totally liberate one from suffering, I would add that wisdom alone cannot lead us without love and allegiance to the will of God.

At this stage the bodhisattva can appear in the world as needed to assist and liberate beings. We see an example of this in the twenty-fifth chapter of the Lotus Sutra. It describes various trials, suffering and impending disaster—including shipwreck, fire, flood, imprisonment, muggers, robbers, demons, lusts and cravings, ignorance and stupidity, wrath and ire, fatal poisons and karmic woes—from which a devotee may be rescued if his thoughts dwell on the power of Kuan Yin and he calls out her name.

Sometimes a transcendent bodhisattva will appear in all his spiritual glory but he can assume whatever form will best allow him to reach those he is trying to help. Again we turn to the twenty-fifth chapter of the Lotus Sutra for an example. The Buddha is asked how the bodhisattva Kuan Yin travels in the world of suffering and how she preaches the dharma to living beings. He describes how Kuan Yin can appear in thirty-three different forms to suit the temperament of the one she is trying to save:

*If there are beings in the land who can be conveyed to deliverance by the body of a Buddha, then to them the Bodhisattva preaches Dharma by displaying the body of a Buddha.*

*To those who can be conveyed to deliverance by the body of the general of the gods, she preaches Dharma by displaying the body of the general of the gods.*

*To those who can be conveyed to deliverance by the body of the wife of an elder, householder, official or Brahman [priest], she preaches Dharma by displaying the body of a woman...*

### THE PARABLE OF THE BURNING HOUSE

Buddhists often tell the parable of the burning house, from the third chapter of the Lotus Sutra, to illustrate the perfection of Skillful Means. This version is told by Nikkyo Niwano in *A Guide to the Threefold Lotus Sutra:*

*In a city in a certain country there was a great elder. His house was enormous but was provided with only a single narrow door. This house was terribly dilapidated, and suddenly one day a fire broke out and began to spread rapidly. The elder's numerous children were all inside. He begged them to come out, but they were all busy at their play. Though it seemed certain that they would be burned, they took no notice and had no urge to escape.*

*The elder thought for a moment. He was very strong*

*and might load them all into some kind of box and bring them out at once. But then he thought that if he did this some might fall out and be burned. So he decided to warn them of the fearsomeness of the fire so that they might come out by themselves.*

*In a loud voice he called to them to come out at once to escape being burned alive, but the children merely glanced up and took no real notice.*

*The elder then remembered that his children all wanted carts, and so he called to them to come out at once because he had the goat carts, deer carts, and bullock carts that they were always wanting.*

*When the children heard this, they finally paid attention and fell all over each other in their rush to get out, and thus they were able to escape from the burning house. The elder was relieved at their safe delivery from harm, and as they began to ask for their carts, he gave each of them not the ordinary carts they wanted but carts splendidly decorated with precious things and drawn by great white bullocks.*[6]

Mahayana Buddhists see the father in this parable as the Buddha. The children are ordinary men and women, and the burning house is life in the world. They see the three carts as the different paths of Buddhism. The costly carriage is the path of the bodhisattva, who would lead all beings to Buddhahood.

## Reflection on the Essence

- In what ways have you used skillful means to help others?

- Recall a time, perhaps when you were a child, perhaps later, when you were led by another's use of skillful means. How did this benefit you?

- Imagine that, like Kuan Yin, you are a transcendent bodhisattva with the ability to appear in whatever form will best allow you to reach someone you desire to help. What form would you take and what challenge would you take on? Visualize the best possible outcome for that challenge or situation.

# 14

*Eighth Bhumi: Acala*
*Immovable Stage*

The eighth bhumi is *Acala,* Immovable (or Irreversible) Stage. This stage is considered so important that it is also referred to as the stage of Perfection, of Birth, of Finality. At this stage, all the Buddhas appear before the bodhisattva and encourage him to attain Buddhahood. They "initiate him into infinite Knowledge"[1] and remind him of his Great Vow in order to persuade him from entering into nirvana.

At this stage the bodhisattva has attained a state of consciousness that we can only conceive of as divine. Sangharakshita says: "He knows in detail the evolution and involution of the universe, the composition of its elements and the nature of its beings. He is now in possession of all the qualities of a Buddha, in consequence of which the possibility of retrogression is permanently precluded."[2]

## THE NON-DUAL NATURE OF REALITY

Sangharakshita explains the manner in which the bodhisattva arrives at this stage that is beyond any possibility of retrogression:

*Broadly speaking, the Bodhisattva becomes Irreversible by the realization of the 'Great Emptiness,' Maha-sunyata.... [He] sees that the distinction between the two—that this is conditioned, this is Unconditioned, this is the world, that's nirvana—...is not ultimately valid....*

*He wakes up from this dream of dualistic thinking into the light, into the reality, of the one mind, the non-dual mind, the non-dual Reality.... He sees the utter absurdity, therefore, of the very idea of individual emancipation, and in this way...the Bodhisattva becomes Irreversible. He can't fall back to individual emancipation because he sees there's no individual emancipation to fall back to.*[3]

### PRANIDHANA-PARAMITA: THE PERFECTION OF THE VOW

From this stage on, the bodhisattva's activities are spontaneous and automatic, arising from his supreme compassion and wisdom. At this stage, along with all the other paramitas, he cultivates the perfection of the Vow *(Pranidhana)*, the eighth paramita.

What impels the bodhisattva forward is his great compassion for those in need of help. He sees that no one else will come to their aid if he does not extend a hand. And in that moment love itself supplies the intensity, the fire that drives the bodhisattva to rescue those in distress.

Love that forgets itself and leaps to save a life creates an opening for the great fire of the Spirit to enter the heart. The strong and virtuous heart is born in that process in which all of God, all of life, all of soul and spirit within the bodhisattva rushes forward to rescue another.

## PAUSING ON THE THRESHOLD OF HEAVEN

The name Kuan Yin is a shortened form of Kuan Shih Yin, which means literally "observing the sounds of the world." According to legend, Kuan Yin was about to enter heaven but paused on the threshold as the cries of the world reached her ears. According to another tradition, aeons ago when Kuan Yin took the bodhisattva vow, she asked to be given a thousand hands and a thousand eyes in order to better assist all life. Her request was instantly fulfilled.

Can we leave this earth while there are yet those in pain? I think not. We would heal their pain as well as its cause, karma, which only leads to more suffering through wrong desire. The healing of our planet requires a teaching and a path that gives us illumination to face the karma we reap. Thus, may we also pause on the threshold between earth and heaven, pursuing our path to Buddhahood through mercy and compassion extended from our heart to every part of life.

## *Reflection on the Essence*

- Reflect on an incident in which you felt that a heavenly being was watching over you, safeguarding you or a loved one, or interceding in your behalf.

- Are there times when you could have used a thousand arms or eyes to help another?

- Consider how praying for the means instead of closing the door to life's demands might allow for miraculous results.

# 15

## Ninth Bhumi: Sadhumati
## Good Thoughts Stage

Now we come to the ninth bhumi, *Sadhumati,* Good Thoughts Stage. At this stage the bodhisattva, as the Preacher of the Law, delivers the Buddha's teaching to all who suffer. His thoughts are good because of the vast analytical knowledge he has gained, through which he knows all the thoughts and desires of men and preaches to them according to the needs of their temperament and through virtually any medium. This stage is also called the Stage of Perfect Wisdom.

### BALA-PARAMITA: THE PERFECTION OF STRENGTH

At this stage the bodhisattva cultivates the perfection of Spiritual Strength and Power *(Bala),* the ninth paramita, to assist in his task of delivering all beings. He experiences many *samadhis.* A samadhi is a state of profound meditation, a mode of concentration. Each samadhi has a definite name, produces specific results, and can be entered into for an almost infinite period of time.

Samadhis can be employed by bodhisattvas in a great many ways for the liberation of souls. This ability is illustrated in a sutra about Manjushri, the Bodhisattva of Wisdom. This version is adapted from Garma Chang's *Treasury of Mahayana Sutras:*

### THE SAMADHI OF DEFEATING DEMONS

*Mañjuśrī had entered the Samadhi of Defeating Demons …[and caused] ten billion demon palaces…[to] become dilapidated, old, and dark.… The demons [likewise] saw their bodies become dull, decrepit, weak, and emaciated, and they had to walk with staffs [and were filled with fear].…*

*…Mañjuśrī again used his miraculous powers to magically produce ten billion devas who appeared before the demons and told them [that all that had befallen them was because of the awesome power of Mañjuśrī's samadhi. The demons then greatly feared Mañjuśrī and begged the devas to save them from danger.]…*

*…[The] devas said to the demons: "Do not be afraid! Do not be afraid! Now you had better go quickly to see Śākyamuni Buddha.… [He] is very kind and compassionate; sentient beings will be eased of their worries and sufferings and be given peace and happiness if they go to take refuge in him.…"*

*...The demon kings and their subjects were over-joyed.... Instantaneously, they arrived at the place where Śākyamuni Buddha was and said in unison, "World-Honored One with great virtue, may you protect and save us.... We would rather accept the names of hundreds of thousands of millions of billions of Buddhas than hear Bodhisattva Mañjuśrī's name alone."...*

*The Buddha told them, "Wait a moment. When Mañjuśrī returns, he will rid you of your shame."...*

*...[When Mañjuśrī returned, Buddha told him,]... "Withdraw your miraculous powers and restore the demons to their original appearance."*

*...Mañjuśrī asked the demons, "Kind sirs, do you really detest this appearance of yours?"*

*The demons answered, "Yes, great sage."*

*Mañjuśrī said to the demons, "If so, now you should detest desire and not attach yourselves to the three realms [the realms of desire]."*

*The demons said, "Yes, great sage. After we hear your good teachings, how dare we disobey?"...*

*Thereupon, Mañjuśrī...restored the demons to their original appearance....*

*[He preached to them the doctrine and] ten thousand demon kings engendered supreme bodhicitta and eighty-four thousand demon subjects were freed from defilements.*[1]

## Reflection on the Essence

- In what way does your understanding of the perfection of bala, *spiritual strength and power,* inspire you?

- If you could employ any samadhi, or mode of concentration, which samadhi would you choose and in what way would you use it?

## 16

*Tenth Bhumi: Dharmamegha*
*Cloud of the Dharma Stage*

ow we come to the tenth and last bhumi, *Dharmamegha*, Cloud of the Dharma Stage. The illustrious sGam.po.pa explained that this stage received its name because the bodhisattva "lets the Dharma fall like rain and extinguishes the very subtle glow of conflicting emotions still held by sentient beings. Another reason is that it is covered by meditative absorption and mantras like the sky with clouds."[1] This is the stage of consecration, in which the bodhisattva has all the attainment, powers and characteristics of a Buddha.

At this stage the bodhisattva is seen in his glorious body sitting upon a celestial lotus adorned with jewels. He is surrounded by countless Buddhas and bodhisattvas. Rays of light issue from his body, illumining the universe and healing sentient beings of pain and misery. Rays of light also stream forth from all the Buddhas, consecrating the bodhisattva as a Buddha. Sangharakshita says of this stage:

> The Bodhisattva, now a Supreme Buddha, has reached the "endless end" of his career.... He performs feats of supernormal power and emanates the countless Transcendental Forms through which, in fulfilment of His Great Original Vow, He will henceforth work for the emancipation of all sentient beings."[2]

### JNANA-PARAMITA: THE PERFECTION OF DIVINE TRANSCENDENT KNOWLEDGE

At this stage the bodhisattva attains the perfection of Divine Transcendent Knowledge *(Jnana)*, the tenth paramita. In Buddhism, jnana refers to pure awareness, primordial wisdom free of divided knowing or conceptual encumbrances.

### THE PERFECT ONENESS OF NOBLE WISDOM

As scholar Dwight Goddard sees it, the culmination of the bodhisattva's path to Buddhahood is

> ...the Perfect Oneness of Noble Wisdom [where] there is no gradation nor succession nor effort. The tenth stage is the first, the first is the eighth, the eighth is the fifth, the fifth is the seventh: what gradation can there be where perfect Imagelessness and Oneness prevail? And what is the reality of Noble Wisdom?... [I]t has no bounds nor

*limits; it surpasses all the Buddha-lands, and pervades...
the heavenly mansions of the Tushita.*[3]

Perhaps the most accurate way to describe this stage, as
well as the path to Buddhahood itself, is with an anecdote
about the Buddha:

> *The Buddha once gathered up a handful of sisu leaves and
> addressed the monks:*
>
> *"Which do you think are the more numerous, monks,
> this small handful of leaves or those in the whole grove?"*
>
> *"Very few in number are the leaves you have taken
> up. Much more in number are those in the whole grove."*
>
> *"Even so, monks, much more in number are those
> things I have discovered but not revealed."*[4]

## *Reflection on the Essence*

- *If you possessed* jnana, *divine transcendent knowledge, and had the attainment of a Buddha, on
  what good would you focus?*

- *Create a vision of earth in which this good has
  come to full realization.*

Chris Foleen

**The Three Bodies of Your Buddha-Nature**
*(Top to bottom: The Dharmakaya, Sambhogakaya and Nirmanakaya.)*

## 17

# The Doctrine of the Trikaya
## (Three Bodies of the Buddha)

Some Buddhists believe that each aspirant to Buddha-hood successively "puts on" three bodies. He begins at the level of the *Nirmanakaya,* called the Body of Trans-formation. This is the physical form of an embodied Buddha, such as Gautama Buddha. It is also the refined, purified body of the striving disciple evolving on the spiritual path. In the Chart, it relates to the lower figure.

The aspirant then puts on the *Sambhogakaya,* the Body of Bliss or the Body of Inspiration. This relates to the Buddha Self, or Higher Self, corresponding to the middle figure in the Chart.

Next, he puts on the *Dharmakaya,* which is called the Body of the Law or Body of First Cause—the timeless, per-manent body of the Buddha. It corresponds to the upper figure in the Chart.

When the three bodies of the Buddha are united and experienced simultaneously, they are known as the *Vajrakaya.* The *vajra* (diamond, adamantine) symbolizes the indestructible nature of the Buddha's wisdom.

The union of these three bodies correlates with the full integration of the soul with her divine image—the Higher (Buddha) Self and God Presence—and her final ascent to her God.

# 18

*Mantras for
Wisdom and Compassion*

When we recite a mantra, we are calling for light to descend from the realm of Spirit to change matter here below. When we know the meaning of a mantra, have an understanding of the enlightened being whose mantra it is, and pour tremendous love to that being through regular repetition of the mantra, we open channels to receiving tremendous love and light in return.

Sangharakshita writes, "By repeating the *mantra* and assuming the *mudra* [ritual gesture] of any Buddha or Bodhisattva one can not only place oneself in correspondence or alignment with the particular order of reality which he personifies but also one can be infused with its transcendental power."[1]

Giving a mudra locks you in to the power and presence of the being whose mudra it is. The presence of an enlightened being is a powerful replica of the fullness of his tangible light body that can be focalized in time and space within the aura of a disciple. Thus a devotee who, in the name of his own God Presence, calls to that being may be blessed with the divine presence of that one.

Giving Buddhist mantras ties us in to the vast cosmic consciousness of all beings who have attained to that degree of God Self-awareness that is called Buddha. This includes the great bodhisattvas of Buddhic attainment, such as Kuan Yin and Manjushri. Buddhist disciples recite mantras to evoke the power and presence of a divine being. In some traditions, devotees use mantras in meditation to help them become one with the deity they are invoking. Many Buddhists will repeat a favorite mantra many hundreds or thousands of times.

All of the Buddhas and great bodhisattvas come in an aura of violet flame. Thus, when we give Buddhist mantras, we are invoking the release of violet flame from these great beings in addition to the other qualities and blessings the specific mantra invokes.

## OM BUDDHA:
### THE POWER OF MANTRA AND MUDRA

To illustrate the power of mantra and mudra, let's take the mantra *Om Buddha*. When we give devotion to the Buddha through the recitation of this mantra, the gentle presence of the Buddha drops over us, affording us an opportunity for our bodies and chakras to be aligned to a greater degree.

Try giving the mantra *Om Buddha* 144 times, pouring love and devotion to the Buddha as you repeat it. Give the earth-touching mudra along with it. This mudra signifies the Buddha's unshakable, steadfast nature; it is associated with Gautama's vanquishing of Mara on the eve of his complete enlightenment.

To form the earth-touching mudra, sit and cup the left hand in the lap. With the right hand cupped and facing toward the floor, symbolically touch the earth. Give this mudra with the sense of being enfolded and overshadowed by Gautama Buddha and with the expectation that all demons who would move against your divine plan will flee.

### *Om Buddha*

#### A VISUALIZATION FOR GIVING MANTRAS

The best position in which to give a mantra is seated in a chair with the spine erect and feet flat on the floor or seated in the lotus or half-lotus posture. Draw in the solar plexus. Visualize yourself in the very heart of the Buddha, and the Buddha in the heart of you. This can be a never-ending visualization: you inside the Buddha, then the Buddha inside of you. See it as an endless interchange of yourself in the being of the Buddha, in the being of God.

*OM AH HUM VAJRA GURU PADMA SIDDHI HUM*

Padma Sambhava, the Lotus-Born One, is revered as the founder of Tibetan Buddhism. His devotees often call him Guru Rinpoche (Precious Guru). Padma Sambhava is said to have been a teacher at the great monastic university in Nalanda, India, in the eighth century. According to Tibetan tradition, Padma Sambhava concealed scriptures containing esoteric teachings, which were discovered by chosen disciples in later centuries.

Padma Sambhava's mantra, known as the *Vajra Guru* mantra, is *Om Ah Hum Vajra Guru Padma Siddhi Hum.* A Vajra Guru is a being who has fully mastered the path of Vajrayana Buddhism. For centuries, devotees of Padma Sambhava have received blessings by invoking this mantra, which means: "Padma Sambhava, who arose from a lotus, please grant me the ordinary and supreme accomplishments, *Hum!*"

Padma Sambhava instructed Yeshe Tsogyal, one of his chief disciples, that his mantra should be used to avert the evils of a coming period of great darkness. His devotees have invoked this mantra to create peace and harmony and to antidote confusion and turmoil. It is a mantra for the era in which we live, a time of the planetary return of karma. Padma Sambhava said that the more times the mantra was given, the greater the benefit would be.

**Om Ah Hum Vajra Guru Padma Siddhi Hum**

## THE INCALCULABLE MERIT OF THE MANTRA
## *OM MANI PADME HUM*

Devotees invoke the power and merciful intercession of Kuan Yin (Avalokiteshvara) with the mantra *Om Mani Padme Hum,* which is translated "Hail to the jewel in the lotus!" The mantra is also said to refer to the Absolute contained within everything. In addition, as with all Buddhist mantras, when we chant any of the Kuan Yin mantras or vows we are also calling forth the transmutative action of the violet flame.

Yeshe Tsogyal recorded Padma Sambhava's teaching on this mantra to the king of Tibet and close disciples. I believe in this teaching with profound conviction because the mantra *Om Mani Padme Hum* is the geometric formula, or mandala, that locks us in to the heart of Kuan Yin. This is Padma Sambhava's teaching:

> OM MANI PADME HUM *is the quintessence of the Great Compassionate One, so the merit of uttering it just once is incalculable....*
>
> *... These six syllables are the quintessence of the mind of noble Avalokiteshvara. If you recite this mantra 108 times a day, you will not take rebirth in the three lower realms. In the following life you will attain a human body and in actuality you will have a vision of noble Avalokiteshvara. If you recite daily the mantra correctly twenty-one times, you will be intelligent and able to retain whatever you learn. You will have a melodious voice and become adept*

*in the meaning of all the Buddhadharma....*

*When someone is afflicted by disease or an evil in-
fluence, compared to any mundane ritual of healing or of
repelling obstacles, the merit of the Six Syllables is much
more effective for warding off obstacles or disease. Compared to any medical treatment or cure, the Six Syllables
are the strongest remedy against sickness and evil.*

*The virtues of the Six Syllables are immeasurable and
cannot be fully described even by the buddhas of the three
times. Why is that? It is because this mantra is the quintes-
sence of the mind of the noble bodhisattva Avalokiteshvara,
who continuously looks upon the six classes of sentient
beings with compassion. Thus, recitation of this mantra
liberates all beings from samsara.*

*Kings and disciples of future generations,*
*Take the Great Compassionate One as your yidam*
[your personal guide to enlightenment].
*Recite the Six Syllables as the essence mantra.*
*Be free from the fear of going to the lower realms.*
*Avalokiteshvara is the destined deity of Tibet,*
*So supplicate him with faith and devotion.*
*You will receive blessings and attainments*
*And be free from doubt and hesitation.*[2]

**Om Mani Padme Hum**

## THE TEN VOWS OF KUAN YIN

The Ten Vows of Kuan Yin are taken from the Great Compassion Heart Dharani Sutra. Like mantras, a *dharani* is a sacred formula. In the Dharani Sutra, Kuan Yin explains that those who wish to "bring forth a heart of great compassion for all beings" should first follow her in making these vows. Recite Kuan Yin's vows as a devout prayer, repeating each one a number of times.

1. *I desire/I vow to quickly know the entire Dharma!*

2. *I desire/I vow to soon attain the eye of perfect wisdom!*

3. *I desire/I vow to quickly save all sentient beings!*

4. *I desire/I vow to soon attain the good and expedient method which leads to full enlightenment!*

5. *I desire/I vow to quickly board the prajna boat!*

6. *I desire/I vow to soon transcend the 'bitter sea'!*

7. *I desire/I vow to quickly attain good discipline, the stability of meditation, and the Way of the Buddha!*

8. *I desire/I vow to soon scale the mountain of Nirvana!*

9. *I desire/I vow to quickly realize the unconditioned!*

10. *I desire/I vow to soon unite with the Dharmakaya!*[3]

*GATE GATE PARAGATE PARASAMGATE BODHI SVAHA*

The mantra *Gate Gate Paragate Parasamgate Bodhi Svaha* is the conclusion of the Heart Sutra. It is translated "Gone, gone, gone beyond, gone wholly beyond—Enlightenment, hail!" or "Proceed, proceed, proceed beyond, proceed completely beyond, be founded in enlightenment." The mantra serves to propel us beyond the illusory self and all illusion, beyond duality, into Reality and the Real Self. It is said to contain the entirety of Perfect Wisdom.

**Gate Gate Paragate Parasamgate Bodhi Svaha**

*OM AH RA PA TSA NA DHIH*

Manjushri's mantra *Om Ah Ra Pa Tsa Na Dhih* is recited to help develop wisdom, memory and an understanding of the scriptures. Wisdom includes wise dominion of ourselves, our aura and our entire being as well as wise dominion of all the affairs entrusted to us and all the individuals who come under our care.

Give this mantra 108 times or in multiples of nine. Following the last repetition, repeat the final syllable as many times as you like. The final syllable, *Dhih,* is the *bija,* or seed syllable, of Manjushri. The essence of a Buddha or great being is concentrated in his bija. By reciting the seed syllable of a fully enlightened being, we access his attainment, aura and momentum.

**Om Ah Ra Pa Tsa Na Dhih**

*OM WAGI SHORI MUM*

Another mantra to Manjushri is *Om Wagi Shori Mum,* which means Hail to the Lord of Speech! That is one of Manjushri's titles. He is the master of eloquence. He uses the word as a tool of liberation to cut through ignorance. We simply cannot entertain the roots of ignorance. We get out of ignorance by an act of will, by the determination and decisions we make about who and what we will be.

This mantra helps you communicate effectively. The voice of the Buddhist god Brahma Sanam-kumara is said to have eight qualities. As we give this mantra, we can ask that our voice have these eight qualities: that the voice be distinct, intelligible, pleasant, attractive, compact, concise, deep and resonant. And I would add a ninth quality: reverent. Reverence for all life, for people, for the God within them.

### Om Wagi Shori Mum

### I AM A BEING OF VIOLET FIRE!
### I AM THE PURITY GOD DESIRES!

The violet flame (introduced in chapter 4) is a spiritual fire of mercy and forgiveness that transmutes negative karma, heals painful memories, and leaves us feeling more joyful and vibrant.

Use the mantra "I AM a being of violet fire! I AM the purity God desires!" and variations on it to invoke mercy, forgiveness, and joy for yourself, loved ones, anyone and everyone, for every situation on earth and for the planet itself. For example:

*I AM a being of violet fire!*
*I AM the purity God desires!*

*My children\* are beings of violet fire!*
*My children are the purity God desires!*

    [\*Give the mantra for anyone and anything, naming individuals, groups, schools, your place of work, and so forth.]

*My heart\* is a chakra of violet fire!*
*My heart is the purity God desires!*

    [\*Give the mantra for each chakra in turn: heart, throat, solar plexus, third eye, soul, crown, base.]

*My body is filled with violet fire!*
*My body is the purity God desires!*

    [Substitute the name of a body part, function, or condition. For example: bones, blood, knees, stomach, brain; memory, vision; health, energy—whatever situation you desire to improve.]

*Earth is a planet of violet fire!*
*Earth is the purity God desires!*

    [Substitute the name of a city, state, region or country.]

Repeat the mantra as many times as you like. While you give it, visualize the violet flame surrounding your entire being and world, surrounding every person, thing and situation you would bless with mercy, forgiveness and joy.

See the violet flame moving through and interpenetrating the spaces between the atoms and thought waves that constitute it. Imagine a roaring violet flame bonfire cleansing and consuming everything less than divine reality, allowing light to shine through.

Try weaving variations on this mantra with a Buddhist mantra. Give a Buddhist mantra nine times, then come back to this mantra or variations on it.

> **I AM a being of violet fire!**
> **I AM the purity God desires!**

## GIVING MANTRAS A TRY

I would ask you to give these mantras a try for a number of days, perhaps thirty-three days. They work profoundly. And the transformation that results will be astounding if you also do all other things that converge in the heart of the bodhisattva.

This includes taking care of the physical body, which is the chalice for the light we receive. Although we are calling for change in the planes of matter, we can't cure ourselves by giving a mantra. The only cure for any situation is the light of God, a grace that is beyond our direct control.

## THE POWER OF DEVOTIONAL PRAYER

Beginning your day with prayer and worship will help you maintain feelings of peace throughout the day no matter what happens. Prayer before retiring at night, for whatever length of time you can give, reinforces that feeling and locks you in to a higher state of consciousness during sleep. In your prayer before sleep, commend to God the problems you are facing in any area of your life. Often you will awaken in the morning with an answer or greater understanding. This is a wonderful ritual, and you develop a momentum on it by practicing it daily.

Once you have begun to use the violet flame to clean up your aura, you will discover that it can create positive change at all levels of your being. The violet flame can free you to progress spiritually, to enjoy the full benefit of positive energy descending from your God Presence, and to realize your highest potential. Uniting with your Higher Self can take many years or even lifetimes. But each time you invoke the violet flame, you are bringing yourself closer to that goal.

The more you give violet-flame mantras, the more you free yourself from limiting conditions. Then you, as an instrument of God's love, are better able to help others. You will find that when others contact your aura, they too will receive healing and upliftment.

### ALL THE GOOD THAT YOU DO IS COUNTED

I invite you to apply each day in your prayers to the Buddhas, great bodhisattvas and enlightened beings. Ask to be shown what to do to be accepted at the next level of your path. Apply yourself to all that precedes and leads to that level until you reach it.

You will know in your inner being, even if your outer being does not know, the rejoicing in continuous striving as you desire to be perfected for only one purpose—that you might heal and deliver and serve all sentient life. With that right motive to the glory of God, you are ascending the ladder.

Trust in the unfailing law of love. All the good that you do is counted.

# $\mathcal{N}otes$

CHAPTER 1 ～ *Buddha-Nature Is Universal*

1. *Ratnagotravibhāga* 1:28, in Edward Conze et al., eds., *Buddhist Texts through the Ages* (1954; reprint, New York: Harper & Row, Harper Torchbooks, 1964), p. 181.
2. Geshe Wangyal, *The Jewelled Staircase* (Ithaca, N.Y.: Snow Lion Publications, 1986), p. 161.
3. *Śūraṅgama Sūtra,* quoted in Lama Anagarika Govinda, *Foundations of Tibetan Mysticism* (New York: Samuel Weiser, 1969), p. 47.
4. *The Śūraṅgama Sūtra,* trans. Lu K'uan Yü (New Delhi: B. I. Publications, 1978), p. 19.
5. Dilgo Khyentse, *The Wish-Fulfilling Jewel: The Practice of Guru Yoga according to the Longchen Nyingthig Tradition* (Boston: Shambhala, 1988), pp. 10, 11.

CHAPTER 2 ～ *The Birth of the Bodhisattva Path in You*

1. Daisetz Teitaro Suzuki, *Outlines of Mahayana Buddhism* (New York: Schocken Books, 1963), p. 329.
2. Nikkyo Niwano, *A Guide to the Threefold Lotus Sutra,* trans. Eugene Langston (Tokyo: Kosei Publishing, 1981), p. 129.
3. See *Densal* 15, no. 1 (Spring/Summer 2000), p. 9.

CHAPTER 3 ～ *Bodhicitta: Awakening the Heart of Enlightenment*

1. Ananda K. Coomaraswamy, *Buddha and the Gospel of Buddhism* (New York: Harper & Row, Harper Torchbooks, 1964), p. 352.
2. Ibid., p. 141.
3. Nagarjuna, *A Discourse on the Transcendentality of the Bodhicitta,* in D. T. Suzuki, *Outlines of Mahayana Buddhism,* p. 298.
4. Ibid., pp. 298–99.
5. Govinda, *Foundations of Tibetan Mysticism,* pp. 273, 274–75.
6. Ibid., pp. 83, 65.
7. Bhikshu Sangharakshita, *A Survey of Buddhism,* rev. ed. (Boulder, Colo.: Shambhala with London: Windhorse, 1980), p. 413.
8. Maha Sthavira Sangharakshita, *The Three Jewels: An Introduction to Buddhism* (1967; reprint, Surrey, England: Windhorse Publications, 1977), p. 179.
9. John Blofeld, *Bodhisattva of Compassion: The Mystical Tradition of Kuan Yin* (Boston: Shambhala, 1977), p. 70.

CHAPTER 4 ～ *Six Practices of Supreme Worship*

1. Sangharakshita, "The Awakening of the Bodhi Heart," from the 1969 lecture series "Aspects of the Bodhisattva Ideal." Sangharakshita's lectures cited in these notes are posted at http://www.freebuddhistaudio.com.
2. Geshe Kelsang Gyatso, *Meaningful to Behold: A Commentary to Shantideva's Guide to the Bodhisattva's Way of Life,* 2d ed. (London: Tharpa Publications, 1986), pp. 45, 48.
3. Ibid., p. 10.
4. Sangharakshita, *A Survey of Buddhism,* pp. 407–8.

CHAPTER 5 ∿ *The Bodhisattva Vow*

1. Lord Maitreya, "Fearless Compassion and the Eternal Flame of Hope," in *Pearls of Wisdom,* vol. 33, no. 1, January 7, 1990 (Gardiner, Mont.: Summit University Press, 1990), p. 11.

2. Bhikshu Sangharakshita, "The Bodhisattva Vow," from the 1969 lecture series "Aspects of the Bodhisattva Ideal."

CHAPTER 6 ∿ *Bodhisattvas Who Would Become a Buddha*

1. Har Dayal, *The Bodhisattva Doctrine in Buddhist Sanskrit Literature* (1932; reprint, Delhi: Motilal Banarsidass, 1970), p. 66.

2. Ibid., p. 57.

3. Shantideva, *Guide to the Bodhisattva's Way of Life: A Buddhist Poem for Today; How to Enjoy a Life of Great Meaning and Altruism,* trans. Neil Elliot under the guidance of Geshe Kelsang Gyatso (Ulverston, England: Tharpa Publications, 2002), pp. 28, 29, 30.

4. "The Sermon at Benares" (excerpt), in Paul Carus, *The Gospel of Buddha: Compiled from Ancient Records* (Chicago, Open Court Publishing, 1915), p. 49.

5. Matt. 23:27.

*The Buddha Replies to the Deva*

1. Carus, *The Gospel of Buddha,* pp. 168–69.

CHAPTER 7 ∿ *First Bhumi: Pramudita, Joyful Stage*

1. Elizabeth Clare Prophet, *Quietly Comes the Buddha* (Gardiner, Mont.: Summit University Press, 2000), p. 23.

2. *Avadāna-çataka,* quoted in Dayal, *The Bodhisattva Doctrine,* pp. 176–77.

3. Eccles. 11:1.

CHAPTER 8 ∼ *Second Bhumi: Vimala, Immaculate Stage*

1. Sangharakshita, *A Survey of Buddhism,* p. 433.

CHAPTER 9 ∼ *Third Bhumi: Prabhakari, Illuminating Stage*

1. Gyatso, *Meaningful to Behold,* pp. 135–36.
2. Dayal, *The Bodhisattva Doctrine,* p. 210.
3. Luke 21:19.
4. "The Sermon on Abuse," in Carus, *The Gospel of Buddha,* pp. 167–68.

CHAPTER 10 ∼ *Fourth Bhumi: Arcismati, Radiant Stage*

1. E. Obermiller, *The Doctrine of Prajna-paramita as Exposed in the Abhisamayalamkara of Maitreya* (Talent, Ore.: Canon Publications, 1984), p. 54.
2. Dayal, *The Bodhisattva Doctrine,* p. 217.
3. Ibid.

CHAPTER 11 ∼ *Fifth Bhumi: Sudurjaya,*
*Very-Difficult-to-Conquer Stage*

1. Bhikshu Sangharakshita, "Altruism and Individualism in the Spiritual Life," from the 1969 lecture series "Aspects of the Bodhisattva Ideal."
2. sGam.po.pa, *The Jewel Ornament of Liberation,* trans. Herbert V. Guenther (Boston: Shambhala, 1959), p. 245.
3. Ibid., p. 187.
4. René Grousset, *In the Footsteps of the Buddha,* quoted in *Maitreya, the Future Buddha,* eds. Alan Sponberg and Helen Hardacre (Cambridge: Cambridge University Press, 1988), p. 11.

*How Long Does It Take to Become a Buddha?*

1. Dayal, *The Bodhisattva Doctrine*, p. 76.
2. *A Dictionary of Buddhist Terms and Concepts* (Tokyo: Nichiren Shoshu International Center, 1983), s.v. "Kalpa."
3. Dayal, *The Bodhisattva Doctrine*, p. 79.

CHAPTER 12 ～ *Sixth Bhumi: Abhimukhi, Face-to-Face Stage*

1. Obermiller, *The Doctrine of Prajna-paramita*, p. 55.
2. *Vimalakirti Nirdesa*, quoted in Beatrice Lane Suzuki, *Mahayana Buddhism: A Brief Outline* (New York: Macmillan, 1969), p. 108.

*Tibetan Prayer to Manjushri*

1. See *Daily Recitations of Preliminaries* (Dharamsala, India: Library of Tibetan Works & Archives).

CHAPTER 13 ～ *Seventh Bhumi: Duramgama, Far-Reaching Stage*

1. B. L. Suzuki, *Mahayana Buddhism*, pp. 69–70.
2. Sangharakshita, *A Survey of Buddhism*, p. 450.
3. H. Wolfgang Schumann, *Buddhism, An Outline of Its Teachings and Schools* (Wheaton, Ill.: Theosophical Publishing House), p. 131.
4. D. T. Suzuki, *Outlines of Mahayana Buddhism*, p. 321.
5. Vimalakirti, quoted in B. L. Suzuki, *Mahayana Buddhism*, p. 72.
6. Niwano, *A Guide to the Threefold Lotus Sutra*, pp. 45–46.

CHAPTER 14 ～ *Eighth Bhumi: Acala, Immovable Stage*

1. Dayal, *The Bodhisattva Doctrine*, p. 290.
2. Sangharakshita, *A Survey of Buddhism*, p. 451.
3. Sangharakshita, "The Bodhisattva Hierarchy," from the 1969 lecture series "Aspects of the Bodhisattva Ideal."

CHAPTER 15 ∼ *Ninth Bhumi: Sadhumati, Good Thoughts Stage*

1. See Garma C. C. Chang, ed., *A Treasury of Mahāyāna Sūtras: Selections from the Mahāratnakūta Sūtra* (University Park, Pa.: Pennsylvania State University Press, 1983), pp. 51–56.

CHAPTER 16 ∼ *Tenth Bhumi: Dharmamegha,*
*Cloud of the Dharma Stage*

1. sGam.po.pa, in Paul Williams, *Mahāyāna Buddhism: The Doctrinal Foundations* (London: Routledge, 1989), p. 213.
2. Sangharakshita, *A Survey of Buddhism,* p. 452.
3. *The Lankavatara Scripture: Self-Realisation of Noble Wisdom,* in *A Buddhist Bible,* ed. Dwight Goddard (Boston: Beacon Press, 1970), p. 343.
4. Lucien Stryk, *World of the Buddha: A Reader* (Garden City, N.Y.: Doubleday & Company, Anchor Books, 1969), pp. lv–lvi.

CHAPTER 18 ∼ *Mantras for Wisdom and Compassion*

1. Sangharakshita, *A Survey of Buddhism,* p. 372.
2. Yeshe Tsogyal, *The Lotus-Born: The Life Story of Padmasambhava,* trans. Erik Pema Kunsang (Kathmandu, Nepal: Rangjung Yeshe Publications, 1998), pp. 195, 196–97.
3. Elizabeth Clare Prophet, *Kuan Yin's Crystal Rosary: Devotions to the Divine Mother East and West* (Gardiner, Mont.: The Summit Lighthouse, 1988), pp. 16–18.

# Selected Bibliography

Blofeld, John. *Bodhisattva of Compassion: The Mystical Tradition of Kuan Yin.* Boston: Shambhala, 1977.

Carus, Paul. *The Gospel of Buddha: Compiled from Ancient Records.* Chicago: Open Court Publishing, 1915.

Chang, Garma C. C., ed. *A Treasury of Mahāyāna Sūtras: Selections from the Mahāratnakūta Sūtra.* University Park, Penn.: Pennsylvania State University Press, 1983.

Conze, Edward, I. B. Horner, David Snellgrove, and Arthur Waley, eds. *Buddhist Texts through the Ages.* New York: Harper & Row, Harper Torchbooks, 1964.

Coomaraswamy, Ananda K. *Buddha and the Gospel of Buddhism.* New York: Harper & Row, Harper Torchbooks, 1964.

Dayal, Har. *The Bodhisattva Doctrine in Buddhist Sanskrit Literature.* 1932. Reprint, Delhi: Motilal Banarsidass, 1970.

Goddard, Dwight, ed. *A Buddhist Bible.* Boston: Beacon Press, 1970.

Govinda, Lama Anagarika. *Foundations of Tibetan Mysticism.* New York: Samuel Weiser, 1969.

Gyatso, Geshe Kelsang. *Meaningful to Behold: A Commentary to*

*Shantideva's Guide to the Bodhisattva's Way of Life.* 2d ed. London: Tharpa Publications, 1986.

Khyentse, Dilgo. *The Wish-Fulfilling Jewel: The Practice of Guru Yoga according to the Longchen Nyingthig Tradition.* Boston: Shambhala, 1988.

Matics, Marion L., trans. *Entering the Path of Enlightenment: The Bodhicaryavatara of the Buddhist Poet Santideva.* London: George Allen & Unwin, 1971.

Naquin, Susan. "The Transmission of White Lotus Sectarianism in Late Imperial China." In Johnson, David, Andrew J. Nathan, and Evelyn S. Rawski. *Popular Culture in Late Imperial China.* Berkeley: University of California Press, 1985.

Nichiren Shoshui International Center. *A Dictionary of Buddhist Terms and Concepts.* Tokyo: Nichiren Shoshui International Center, 1983.

Niwano, Nikkyo. *A Guide to the Threefold Lotus Sutra.* Tokyo: Kosei Publishing, 1981.

Obermiller, E. *The Doctrine of Prajna-paramita as Exposed in the Abhisamayalamkara of Maitreya.* Talent, Ore.: Canon Publications, 1984.

Prophet, Elizabeth Clare. *Quietly Comes the Buddha: Awakening Your Inner Buddha-Nature.* Gardiner, Mont.: Summit University Press, 1998.

Sangharakshita, Bhikshu. *A Survey of Buddhism.* Rev. ed. Boulder, Colo.: Shambhala with London: Windhorse, 1980.

Sangharakshita, Maha Sthavira. *The Three Jewels: An Introduction to Buddhism.* Surrey, England: Windhorse Publications, 1977.

Santideva. *Siksa-Samuccaya: A Compendium of Buddhist Doctrine.* Trans. Cecil Bendall and W. H. D. Rouse. Delhi: Motilal Banarsidass, 1971.

Schumann, H. Wolfgang. *Buddhism: An Outline of Its Teachings and Schools.* Wheaton, Ill.: Theosophical Publishing House, 1973.

sGam.po.pa. *The Jewel Ornament of Liberation.* Trans. Herbert V. Guenther. Boston: Shambhala, 1959.

Shantideva and Geshe Kelsang Gyatso. *Guide to the Bodhisattva's Way of Life: A Buddhist Poem for Today—How to Enjoy a Life of Great Meaning and Altruism.* Trans. Neil Elliot. Ulverston, England: Tharpa Publications, 2002.

Sponberg, Alan, and Helen Hardacre, eds. *Maitreya, the Future Buddha.* Cambridge: Cambridge University Press, 1988.

Stryk, Lucien. *World of the Buddha: A Reader.* Garden City, N.Y.: Doubleday and Company, Anchor Books, 1969.

*The Śūraṅgama Sūtra.* Trans. Lu K'uan Yü. New Delhi: B. I. Publications, 1978.

Suzuki, Beatrice Lane. *Mahayana Buddhism: A Brief Outline.* New York: Macmillan, 1969.

Suzuki, Daisetz Teitaro. *Outlines of Mahayana Buddhism.* New York: Schocken Books, 1963.

Tsogyal, Yeshe. *The Lotus-Born: The Life Story of Padmasambhava.* Trans. Erik Pema Kunsang. Kathmandu, Nepal: Rangjung Yeshe Publications, 1998.

Wangyal, Geshe. *The Jewelled Staircase.* Ithaca, N.Y.: Snow Lion Publications, 1986.

Williams, Paul. *Mahāyāna Buddhism: The Doctrinal Foundations.* London: Routledge, 1989.

## TO LEARN MORE ABOUT THE BUDDHIC ESSENCE:

*Quietly Comes the Buddha:*
*Awakening Your Inner Buddha-Nature*
*by Elizabeth Clare Prophet*
Prose, poetry, meditations and prayers for developing your Buddhic nature and cultivating its qualities known as the Ten Perfections.

### We Also Recommend from the
## MYSTICAL PATHS OF THE WORLD'S RELIGIONS:

*The Buddhic Essence*
*by Elizabeth Clare Prophet*   1 DVD
Engaging, heartfelt teachings from Mrs. Prophet's original lecture.

*Kabbalah: Key to Your Inner Power*
*by Elizabeth Clare Prophet*

*Roots of Christian Mysticism*
*by Elizabeth Clare Prophet*   3-DVD set

www.MysticalPaths.org

### *for* MORE TEACHINGS
## FROM ELIZABETH CLARE PROPHET:

**iTunes, YouTube, Podcasts, Videos**
*Listen. Watch. Share. Subscribe.*
www.SummitLighthouse.org/Multimedia.html

Summit University Press books and products are also available at fine bookstores worldwide and at your favorite online bookseller. A wide selection of Summit University Press books has been translated into a total of 29 languages worldwide.

## SUMMIT UNIVERSITY 🕭 PRESS®
63 Summit Way, Gardiner, MT 59030-9314 USA
Tel: 1-800-245-5445 or 406-848-9500
Fax: 1-800-221-8307 or 406-848-9555
*Se habla espanol.*
E-mail: info@SummitUniversityPress.com
www.SummitUniversityPress.com
www.SummitLighthouse.org

ELIZABETH CLARE PROPHET is a world-renowned author. Among her bestselling titles are *Fallen Angels and the Origins of Evil, The Lost Years of Jesus, Reincarnation: The Missing Link in Christianity, Kabbalah: Key to Your Inner Power,* from the Mystical Paths of the World's Relgions series, and her Pocket Guides to Practical Spirituality series, which includes *Your Seven Energy Centers, Karma and Reincarnation, The Story of Your Soul,* and *Violet Flame to Heal Body, Mind and Soul.*

She has pioneered techniques in practical spirituality, including the creative power of sound for personal growth and world transformation.

A wide selection of her books have been translated into a total of 29 languages worldwide.

Mrs. Prophet retired in 1999 and is now living in Montana's Rocky Mountains. The unpublished works of Mark L. Prophet and Elizabeth Clare Prophet continue to be published by Summit University Press.

www.ElizabethClareProphet.org